Cretin '61
A Class Memoir

A Christian Brothers, All- Boys Military School
Joe Delmont

Delmont Books LLC
25 Dorset Road
Mendota Heights, Minnesota, 55118
United States of America
www.DelmontBooks.com

joe@delmontbooks.com

Copyright © 2022 Delmont Books LLC. All rights reserved.

ISBN 978-1-937391-74-4

Printed in the United States of America
Cover photos and facing photo used with permission of Cretin-Derham Hall, 2022.

CRETIN CLASS OF '61

What Was It Like To Be Part of This Group?

Cretin '61 was founded in 1871 as an all-male, blue-collar, Catholic, military high school, for day students, one that emphasized physical discipline and man-to-man directness to teach personal responsibility and excellence in athletics, academics, and career development as we grew from boys to men. This school ceased to exist when Cretin dropped mandatory JROTC and merged with Derham Hall High School. This book is a snapshot of our school days in 1957-1961. CHS

Table of Contents

Acknowledgments . . . . **vi**

The Beginning **1**

Quotes To Guide Us **3**

Prologue **5**

Day One. Cretin Culture Begins **9**

Making The Grade **13**

The Time of Our Lives **17**

Another World **19**

Tuition **25**

Traditions **29**

Hitchhiking **33**

Pranks and Urban Myths **37**

Senior Class Trip **41**

Discipline **49**

Military **51**

    Instructors **55**

    Military Activities **59**

    Crack Drill Squad **63**

    Rifle Range **67**

Christian Brothers **69**
Lay Faculty. **97**
Athletics **101**
    Coaches **107**
    Game Reports **119**
    Scoreboard, 1960-61 . . . . **127**
    Intramural Sports. **131**
Academics/Science **133**
Girls/Schools **137**
Social Scene **141**
The Last Word. **157**
Appendix **159**
    In Memoriam. **159**
    Graduating Class **163**
    National Honor Society **167**
    Awards **168**
    Contributors. **170**
    Sponsors. **171**

Acknowledgments

This book could not have been completed without the dedication and hard work of many people. In any list of Acknowledgements such as this, someone significant usually is left out. At the risk of making such an error, it's still important to identify those who made major contributions to this project. So, in no particular order, thank you to…

Bobbie Delmont, my wife, for her constant encouragement, determined research, and diligent proofreading. She's been proofing my writing for more than 50 years, and she's saved me from embarrassment many times.

Mal Scanlan, for his project coordination and demonstrated ability to bring together players from all segments of our class.

Mike Wold, for applying his skill and the experience gained in publishing our outstanding 50th Anniversary Book to this project.

Paul Ossmann, for his leadership and problem solving skills in successfully guiding this project, and for his detailed editorial assistance.

Richard Peacha, for his 24/7 enthusiasm and excitement for this project. And for his success in digging out data on Catholic grade schools of the 1960s.

Bill Kuhns, for reading and proofing this manuscript to improve its content and readability.

Bro. Bob Walsh, for his assistance in digging through the archives of the Christian Brothers at Cretin to produce biographical profiles of those who contributed most to our class.

MSgt. (Ret.) Dave Berrisford, Cretin Class of 1987, who educated me to Cretin's military history.

Peggy Schafer, the dedicated professional in the Cretin-Derham Hall Alumni Office, who provided historical details and data and many hours of assistance when we needed them.

Don Wolkerstorfer, for supplying additional articles when called upon, and who provided a keen editing eye to correct my typing and factual errors.

Minnesota Historical Society

St. Paul Pioneer Press newspaper.

Minneapolis StarTribune newspaper.

Highland Villager newspaper.

Archdiocese of St. Paul

One Last Note: Some of the characters in this memoir have gone unnamed to protect the innocent. Many of the activities of high school boys are ones that senior citizens may not want their future generations to review, but still the events represent the activities and culture of our day, so we've included them, sans personal identifiers. We know you'll understand. **CHS**

The Beginning

This book was conceived in August 2021 at Mancini's, a St. Paul bar on West Seventh Street, where we often hung out and that day were celebrating our Sixtieth Class Reunion. At that time, there were only about 165 survivors of our original class of 249, and over drinks we shared our memories, as you do at high school reunions.

In between drinks, Mal Scanlan reminded us we were one of the greatest Cretin classes ever. Cretin's Christian Brothers and lay staff prepared us to take on the world and accomplish great things in law, medicine, arts, science government and business. Just look at the number of PhDs, physicians, attorneys, business executives, military officers, government leaders, professional athletes and artists produced by Cretin. Our 50th Anniversary Book edited by Mike Wold contains many of the details.

As we talked and drank and laughed and remembered, someone suggested we gather those memories while there was still time and publish them. So, that's what we did.

We met in discussion groups during several afternoon meetings at Cretin to share and build on those special times.

It's quite amazing, really, how often someone would say something like, "Do you remember…." And another would add, "Yes, and there was another time when…"

We recorded those discussions, compiled and edited the transcripts, called others across the country, who couldn't participate in person, added their input and produced this book.

Our goal was simply to share the memories of what it was like to live through four years of development as we grew into men, guided by the strict discipline of the Christian Brothers in an all-boys military training ground. It wasn't always easy, but it certainly was effective and memorable.

We wrote this book for ourselves, but even if you weren't part of the Class of '61, we hope you appreciate those days, and we hope you enjoy visiting our memories of those times as much as we did in reliving them. **CHS**

—The Editors

Quotes To Guide Us

"In the twilight of our lives, we are judged on one thing—charity."
—Brother K. Mark

"Let us remember that we are in the holy presence of God."
—Class Prayer

"Mary Queen of Victory, Pray for Us."
—Team Pre-Game Prayer

"You are responsible for your actions, and there are immediate consequences for those actions."
—Class Theme

"In each of us there is a private hope and dream which fulfilled can be translated into benefit for everyone. One person can make a difference, and everyone should try."
—John F. Kennedy

Prologue

September 1, 2021

A Unique Time

Jim Stewart had been struggling with a broken arm since the third football game of the year against Fargo Shanley his senior year in 1960 and he wanted the cast gone so he could start playing hockey. His buddy, Gary Droubie, was more than willing to help by cutting off the cast with a large pair of scissors, as the two were just hanging out one day at Gary's house. Stew's Dad wasn't impressed with Gary's medical treatment. Friends.

Mike Cardinal arrived early the first day of class in Advisory 113 and was anxiously awaiting the beginning of school when Prof. Hank Conroy arrived. "Prof. Conroy took one look at me and whacked me in the head. 'That's so you don't act like your older brothers did.'" Discipline.

"Let us remember we are in the holy presence of God," recited every 15 minutes every day. Religion.

Rich Peacha, dubbed the Bear because he had a black beard at the age of 12, used his good looks to buy beer for his underage classmates. They drank it on lovely summer evenings while relaxing on the shore of the Mississippi River. More Friends.

Mal Scanlan refused—yes, just refused, for no good reason—to memorize a poem in one of Bro. K. Mark's English classes. It was a dumb move because it kept Scanlan from playing in an important hockey game after school. His Dad saw to it that the poem was memorized by 7:00 the next morning. Responsibility.

"You are the best." The mantra that was drilled into us from Day One. The Best, academically. The Best, athletically. The Best, as men.

Cretin JROTC-1960, was one of the largest and most successful high school JROTC programs in the country. Military.

This was a special time for Cretin High School and the Class of '61. Cretin was founded in 1871, 151 years ago, and the Class of '61 is celebrating its sixty-first commencement anniversary in 2022.

This book commemorates these events. It's a history of Cretin's important milestones, and at the same time, it's a snapshot of a unique time in American education and American society—a time that no longer exists.

It was a time at Cretin of mandatory military training and man-to-man physical discipline run by Christian Brothers where the consequences of an unacceptable act were immediate and stinging.

Cretin High School. Class of 1961. This is our story. But it can be your story, too, even if you're part of another Cretin generation or if you simply want to know what it was like to attend one of America's premier all-boys military schools based in St. Paul in 1960.

As we begin this project, it's been 65 years since we first walked through the double doors of Cretin High School on Hamline and Randolph avenues in St. Paul, Minnesota.

Although the school has been known as Cretin-Derham Hall since 1987, when it merged with Derham Hall girls school, it will always be known to our class as, simply, Cretin High School, the all-boys military school run by the Christian Brothers.

The school was founded as Cretin, and that's how we remember it. Cretin.

The Army's junior Reserve Officers Training Program (JROTC) was launched in 1917, and Cretin at that time became one of the first of only a handful of participating JROTC non-boarding schools offering grades 9-12 in the country. **CHS**

Day One.
Cretin Culture Begins

He grew up in the neighborhood and spent eight years at Holy Spirit Grade School which shared a parking lot with Cretin High School in St. Paul. Now, he was looking forward to enrolling at Cretin—he was an athlete, and he knew the Christian Brothers. He'd hung with them for years, while he was running through the neighborhood and playing games at the school. They were friendly, and he could hardly wait to share his high school days with them.

Then, it was The First Day. But not exactly what he was expecting. "I remember that day. Walking through the double doors and seeing two Christian Brothers—standing there in their black robes, with their arms crossed on their chests, scowling. Oh, oh. This wasn't good. These weren't the same guys I had seen on the playground.

"After years of having my way with the Catholic nuns at Holy Spirit, I could see this was going to be different. I could feel it, and I didn't know if I liked it. What had I gotten myself into?"

He couldn't back out. There were generations of family who had gone before him. There was a family tradition to uphold. But, dang, it didn't look good.

The Brothers had always been friends. "I mean, they had really been friendly. Oh s_ _ _, this is a different deal. The sisters had no shot, they just couldn't handle eighth grade boys. These guys looked different. Welcome to Cretin High School. I thought it would be easy because I was familiar with the physical part of the school, more like grade school, with my friends, the Brothers." Wrong.

Day One, September 1957, at Cretin. That's how one classmate described it. I don't remember much about that first day, but it was burned into the memories of a lot of other Cretin men.

Pat McLaughlin: "I know I was afraid   I walked in and looked around and said, 'Holy s_ _ _, this is out of my league. What am I doing? It was intimidating, and I was a lucky one because there was a bunch of Markers (Guys from near-by St. Mark's Grade School, one of the city's largest Catholic grade schools.) and I had company at least, a few friendly faces. I was scared to death, excited and scared at the same time. I don't think I'd ever seen Brothers before I walked in. It was scary and it didn't get any better for two years."

Don Wolkerstorfer had a better first impression of the Brothers: "I remember the first time I came to Cretin in the hallway, maybe the first day of school. Brother Gabriel met me in the hall and said, hello to me by my name. I was impressed."

On the first day, Mike Wold walked down the halls and saw the class pictures of his dad and uncles. "I felt they were looking down at me, saying, 'Glad you're here, Mike, but failure is not an option!'"

Not so impressive was the uniform distribution process. First Sgt. Willis McIver, an active duty Army instructor, when handing out pants to a freshman, who was complaining about the fit, said, "I'm not selling you these pants, I'm issuing them. This is what you get. Good-by."

Brother Wilfred, who served as the school's quarter master in charge of uniforms, was no easier. Known to hand out waist size 38" pants to those who measured size 34", Brother would say, "Those pants fit. Take them." Where's my Mom when I need her?

One newbie entered the front doors and met an upper-classman, who tried to sell him a Pool Pass. "Then you won't have to stand in line when you get to the pool.".... Cretin doesn't have a pool. It doesn't have an elevator, either, so the elevator passes were a scam, as well.

And so it begins. Our four years at Cretin High school.

This is our story, the Cretin Class of 1961. **CHS**

Making The Grade

There was so much pressure, even before the first day of class: To pass The Test—the Entrance Exam. To be accepted by The Brothers. Questions swirled through our heads: Would I continue the generations of our family to attend Cretin? Would I be the first of our family to make the grade? Would I make the goal and reach the Citadel of Cretin that the Sisters had set for us? Would I make the grade school proud? Or would I fail to meet everyone's expectations? Please, God, help me in The Test.

"I thought I had done well on the famous entrance exam," says Mike Wold, "until I was talking with my friend Jim Allen, a very bright guy, and we started discussing the questions and answers as we walked to the bus. Whoops! Obviously, I had goofed up The Test, and I was sure I would not be accepted, much to my shame and the embarrassment of my family."

(Mike's fears turned out not to be true. He was accepted and eventually was selected for the National Honor Society and won academic scholarships to St. Mary's College and St. John's University.)

Jim Stewart, who went on to have an outstanding four-year career at Cretin playing football, hockey and baseball, remembers that his test was so stressful he almost couldn't complete the enrollment process. He had transferred from Grand Forks the first day of eighth grade and didn't have many friends in town.

"Cretin was totally unfamiliar to me until about a month before The Test," Stewart recalls. "I was certain I would attend Murray High where all my friends were going, and I was pleased about that. Then, I found out that I lived outside the attendance area and would be going to Ramsey High School in Roseville without my friends." Bad.

"I was the only one from Holy Childhood Grade School that I knew of in that situation. I began to check into Cretin. Sometime late winter I was recruited by the Holy Childhood basketball team to play in the end of the year tournament held at Cretin. We actually won our division. Following the last game, Brother Josephus came up to me and asked if I was interested in Cretin. Unlike everyone else at Holy Childhood (there were 20 or so who took The Test that Saturday morning), it was a nightmare for me. It seemed like there were 800 eighth graders jammed into the Gym/cafeteria (actually, there were about 600).

"I completely botched The Test. Wasn't able to finish. I found out later that I had test anxiety. I was certain that I would not be selected, and I would be going to Ramsey.

"After I was selected (much to my surprise), I found out Sister Louise, my eighth grade teacher/Principal had written a letter strongly recommending me. In mid-May I received The Letter from Cretin, telling me I had been accepted. I thought I had died and gone to Heaven. Only four from our school who had taken The Test were selected—Dick Harren, Bill Englund, Dan Rask, and Dick Warren."

So, this was now our world: studies, athletics, military, White, middle-class Catholic boys, facing the Christian Brothers and learning discipline, ethics, and personal responsibility.

We didn't know there was another world outside of Cretin. **CHS**

The Time of Our Lives

Mike Cardinal remembers his introduction to Prof. Hank Conroy. "It was the first day of school and I was one of the only guys in Advisory 113. I was talking with another newbie when Prof. Conroy came in and headed in my direction.

"He took one look at me and asked me if I had older brothers who went to Cretin. When I answered, 'Yes,' he smacked me in the head, and knocked me right out of my desk. 'That's so you don't start out like your brothers.' And that's not the last time he hit me, either." Discipline with a beat.

The 10-year period, 1955-1965, was the time of our lives—grade school graduation, high school, college, profession. It also was a very special time in America.

While we were growing up in this time, America and St. Paul-Minneapolis were changing dramatically, too. Politically. Racially. Scientifically. Socially.

This book is about our four years at Cretin. But it's also about the times we lived in and the social forces that helped mold us into the men we are today, even though we might not have recognized these times outside of our school days.
CHS

Another World

We grew up in the 1950s and 1960s. Times were different then, not better, not worse, just different. Very different. But the same, too, in many ways. Consider the decade, 1955-1965 during which we attended Cretin.

In the early 1950s, while we were in grade school, before we came to Cretin in 1957, we talked about The Bomb. Nuclear war with Russia was a given, and we had regular bomb drills in grade school—we learned to cower under our desks to protect ourselves from the bomb blasts and nuclear radiation that we knew were soon to come.

This hiding tactic offered no protection whatsoever, but it taught us to be afraid. Very afraid. And it taught us to look for the yellow and black diamond Civil Defense signs that defined CD bomb shelters. We even had a shelter in the Cretin basement.

Army Master Sergeant (Retired) Dave Berrisford, an instructor at Cretin-Derham Hall, found an access door to the shelter from the Military Office, about 2009, and investigated.

In the CD shelter crawl space were stored first aid kits, bandages, iodine, 55 gallon drums of water, and plastic buckets full of hard candy. The crawl space was about 30 x 40 feet and about four feet high. It was purely a storage area for supplies. Pipes in the space are wrapped with asbestos, so there's no access to the space today.

Russia launched Sputnik, the first satellite to circle the globe, in 1957, the year we graduated from grade school and started at Cretin. Sputnik jumpstarted the space race that drove a feverish new U.S. emphasis on math and science education.

Two years later, the Soviets landed Luna2 on the moon. America responded, landing a crew on the moon in 1969.

Catholic education was booming during our Cretin years. In the St. Paul area, there were more than 40 Catholic grade schools with a total student population exceeding 27,000 pupils, or some 12,000 boys. There were more than 600 eighth grade boys competing for 249 spots in the spring of 1956 for the 1961 Class at Cretin. Only the best of the best, students and athletes made that cut.

Our Decade was a time of intense racial conflict in America, but we had no racial conflicts at Cretin because we had no Blacks in our class. This was the result of simple demographics, not a school segregation policy.

At that time, only about 11 percent of the total population of Ramsey County were Black. If you consider that only a small percentage of that population were high school age students who were willing and able to pay for a private school education at a Catholic military institute, statistically we should have had only one or two Blacks in our class of 249 students.

At the same time, St. Paul had a thriving and dynamic Black community in the Rondo neighborhood, although that was soon to be destroyed to make room for the I-94 freeway. The Rondo area generally extended from

Summit-University on the south to University Avenue on the north and West to Hamline Avenue from the Cathedral area. The neighborhood's Central High School provided excellent academic and athletic opportunities for its students. Why pay for Cretin when you could go to Central, your neighborhood school, for free?

The landmark Supreme Court decision of Brown vs. Board of Education in 1954 paved the way for integration of America's schools, from elementary to college.

Following the Brown decision, America saw a defiant response from Southern Whites in 1955 exemplified by the torture and murder of 14-year-old Emmet Tills in Mississippi and the beatings and murders of three white civil rights workers, also in Mississippi that same year.

America witnessed federal troops enforcing school integration in Mississippi and Alabama in 1965. White Gov. George Wallace refused to meet with Martin Luther King Jr. and 30,000 civil rights demonstrators in Montgomery, Alabama. At the same time, Mississippi Gov. Ross Barnett said he would send help to prevent the federal government from "running over and stomping" local government. State's rights vs. the federal government.

Also that year, Rosa Parks, a Black lady, refused to give up her bus seat to a White passenger in Montgomery and was arrested, sparking mass protests and sit-ins across the South.

Medgar Evers, a Black civil rights worker, was assassinated for his efforts in Jackson, Mississippi, in 1955.

The War on Poverty legislation was passed in 1964, partly to honor President John F. Kennedy, who was assassinated in November 1963. The Civil Rights Act of 1964 outlaws discrimination on the basis of race or color.

Martin Luther King, Jr., the Black preacher and civil rights leader, who was active from 1955 until he was assassinated in 1968, led a protest March on Washington of some 250,000 people in 1963.

Dr. King's "I Have a Dream" speech, at the March is one of the most dramatic and frequently quoted speeches in the English language. On March 25, 1965, "Bloody Sunday," Dr. Martin Luther King, Jr., led an estimated 600 civil rights marchers from Selma, AL, to Montgomery, AL, to protest the killing of civil rights worker John Smith. The marchers were attacked by police with night sticks and police dogs and sprayed with fire hoses. Read more about these days in Wikipedia.

Two weeks later, 25,000 marchers protected by federal marshals crossed the Edmund Pettus Bridge, and walked for five days from Selma to Montgomery, 50 miles away.

Viola Liuzzo, a White woman was shot gunned to death by three Klansmen in March 1965 in Alabama.

Ghetto Riots raged across the country from 1964 – 1969. The so-called Ghetto Riots of the Sixties also called ghetto rebellions, race riots or negro riots, left more than 200 dead and 20,000 imprisoned as cities burned from California to New York and Minneapolis and Detroit to Louisville and Miami.

As we were working our way through Cretin and learning the basics of military tactics and the tricks to cleaning an M1 rifle without losing a thumb in its firing mechanism, other teenagers were killing and being killed in Vietnam, a war that started about 1955 and dragged on into 1975, killing 17,000 American servicemen in 1968. More than 303,000 Americans were wounded in the war.

President John F. Kennedy was assassinated in Dallas Nov. 22, 1963, and his brother, Robert F. Kennedy was assassinated in 1968 in Los Angeles during his run for the presidency.

Americans watched the Vietnam war and the aftermath of the assassinations on the new black and white televisions in our living rooms. Shocking.

TV was still so new in 1960 that retailers had to work hard to sell the fancy attraction. In 1960, Butwinick Bros. Furniture in St. Paul offered an Admiral brand 21 inch, all wood, black and white console TV for $199, complete with an in-home demonstration! TV was still so new consumers actually had to be shown how it could improve our in-home entertainment experience.

In 1960, the average hourly wage was about $2.50, and the average annual income was slightly less than $5,000. Today, American workers are paid an average of $26.92 an hour and the average annual income is about $71,000. A dollar in 1960 would be worth $28 in today's dollars in purchasing power. Today, that $199 TV would cost you about $1,900, but for that price, at Best Buy, you could take home a smart 75-inch, flat screen, Ultra High Density color TV. Maybe consumers are much better off today.

As we prepared to graduate in May 1961, we read reports from Montgomery, Alabama, that steel helmeted national guardsmen "with fixed bayonets" enforced martial law and scattered "a howling mob that tried to overwhelm federal marshals protecting a Negro church mass meeting.

The Associated Press reported that troops were given "sweeping powers" to restore order throughout the city where 20 persons were beaten in rioting the previous day. The surging mob, said the report, was finally forced back after officers tossed tear gas bombs.

As we worried about final exams, the Twilight Parade and the Junior Record Hop, people in Alabama and Mississippi were dying over integration, civil rights and states' rights, opposing the federal government.

One lady from Our Lady of Peace (OLP) high school says, "Compared to our kids and grandkids today, we lived in a bubble. And if you talked about the world—I had no idea what was going on in the world. All I knew was my life and my friends and the guys and their friends, and there was just a big group of us. And we couldn't afford to do anything, so we just hung out."

We were insulated from the real world, for the most part, in our cocoon at Cretin. **CDH**

Tuition

Most of the men in our class paid their tuition by working jobs at school and working at other jobs after school and during the summer.

Larry Jandrich remembers setting pins in a bowling alley for eleven cents a line when he wasn't working at Dannecker's Grocery for 75 cents an hour.

Every Monday morning Larry would show up at the Cretin business office to make a tuition payment. Mrs. Pierson would take his small payment and apply it to his account.

Jerry Filla worked at Kormann's Grocery, but he should have had Larry negotiate his compensation. Jerry made only 35 cents an hour and four years later when he finished at Cretin, he was making only 50 cents per hour!

I think Jerry may have gotten some of that money back, though, because the grocer, Phil Kormann, ended up being Jerry's client when Jerry practiced law. Jerry was very good at building relationships. He was our class president every year, and he was voted Most Popular in our senior year.

Despite his great record at Cretin, there were a few bumps in Jerry's academic career. He skipped sixth grade, so he was the youngest in his class from then on. He actually was kicked out of St. Mary's Grade School for conflicts with some of the older guys, but later was readmitted.

Jerry's youth showed up more than once at inopportune times during his military activities at Cretin. When commanding the troops as commander of the Fifth Battalion, young Mr. Filla's voice occasionally cracked when shouting commands.

Ron Bierbaum may have had the most unusual summer job—he worked for his dad, who managed Calvary Cemetery, on the burial detail.

"I cut grass, too," remembers Ron. "At least it was outdoor work and it helped me pay my tuition and graduate." Even more important, Ron became the first member of his family to go to college.

John Biebel was another alley rat, setting pins at bowling alleys in South St. Paul. He also spent many hours washing dishes in restaurants along Concord Avenue in SSP to pay his tuition.

Gary Francis and Bob Hanson worked their way through hospital kitchens, Gary, who later became an internationally-recognized cardiologist, did so with a bit less drama than Bob.

Let Bob tell his story: "I was mopping up in the kitchen one day and at one point I had to rinse out my mop. I spotted a big pot of dirty water and started to clean my mop in it. Bad move. The cook ran screaming at me that I was going to ruin her whole batch of soup!! The "dirty water" was the soup for the day!!

"It all worked out, though, because I got transferred out of the kitchen next day to the cafeteria, which was much better duty."

I washed cars in the St. Paul Hotel garage. It was a sweatshop, literally. I had to wear rubber waders and a heavy rubber apron to keep dry, but all that gear did was to make me sweat like a dog. And the rich folks who stayed at the hotel were never satisfied with the job I did, anyway!

The guys who worked off part of their tuition by helping in the school cafeteria may have had the best deal of all of us. They grabbed extra food and they handed out extra portions of the good stuff to their buddies. They were very popular guys.

Gary Droubie, who worked in the cafeteria all four years, says, "I brown-bagged it like most of the guys, but I usually had eaten my lunch by about 10:30, so I had to get more food from the cafeteria at lunchtime." He didn't pay for the cafeteria meals. And he was a good source of extra portions for many of the guys who came through the line, especially when Sloppy Joes were being served.

Tuition varied by year, but in 1963 it cost $190.00 plus fees for a freshman to attend Cretin for one year. Seniors had to pay $235.00 plus fees.

Annual tuition at Cretin in 2021 was $15,000.

In 1963, Brother H. Richard, the principal, wrote to parents telling them about the tuition hike, saying it was "impossible to operate the school on a financially sound basis without an increase in tuition."

At the same time, Bro. Richard announced a new pricing scheme for the cafeteria. Moving forward, a full plate lunch would be 50 cents and a smaller plate would be 30 cents.

Military uniforms were purchased by each Cadet. A jacket cost $15.75; trousers, $17.00; white gloves, 55 cents; shirts, $3.75; cap $2.50; and a black belt, 75 cents.

Sales were all cash.

Cretin life often was a family affair, and it's not unusual to find many, many generations of families graduating from Cretin.

Many of the oldest and most respected St. Paul names such as McQuillan, Scanlan, Haigh, Mauer, Salmen, Shiely,

Votel, and Laramy have sent generations of boys to Cretin. Girls, too, following the 1987 merger with Derham Hall.

It's common to hear stories of expensive Sam Brown belts and sabers being passed down from generation to generation. **CHS**

Traditions

When you walk the halls of Cretin, you sense the traditions going back to the school's founding in 1871. Cretin is one the earliest JROTC schools in the United States, having been authorized as a unit of the Reserve Officer Training Corps in February 1919. Look at the photos of generations of Cretin graduates guarding the walls and read the names listed there. You'll get the idea.

"I will never forget the pictures of all of the classes on those walls at Cretin," says Mike Wold. "My dad, four uncles and four cousins attended Cretin. As I went by their pictures, I was inspired by them to hang in there even on days that were not going well. I wanted to carry the standard for our family, and I was so proud to be at the graduation ceremony in the St. Paul Auditorium."

Tradition was an important part of the culture at Cretin.

> Tradition, Tradition! Tradition!
> Tradition, tradition! Tradition!
> Who, day and night, must scramble for a living,
> Feed a wife and children, say his daily prayers?
> And who has the right, as master of the house,
> To have the final word at home?
> The Papa, the Papa! Tradition.
> **—Fidler on the Roof**

Cretin High School was founded by Bishop Joseph Cretin in 1871 and that's when the traditions began for generations of Cretin men. The traditions of teaching young boys to become responsible men. From the first day, it was all about Traditions.

The Tradition of personal responsibility.

The Tradition of man-to-man discipline and mentoring.

The Tradition of excellence in academics and athletics.

The Tradition of being the best. "You are the best."

We began hearing these messages when we first walked through the impressive double doors on Hamline Avenue. Today, whenever two of us get together, it's still part of the conversation. Traditions.

Many alumni are dedicated to Cretin, and Mal Scanlan used this affection in his development and fund raising efforts. Joe Shiely II, '36, was one of those alumni who used to call Scanlan regularly.

"He never said Hello or Good-by," recalls Mal. "Just said what he had to say and was gone. One time, after he sold his company, he called me. 'Scanlan, Shiely. Come on over. I have a check for you. For tuitions. And if it happens to go to a couple of speedy halfbacks, that's okay, too.' Click." The check was for $600,000. **CHS**

Hitchhiking

One of the differences between Cretin and St. Thomas Academy (STA) is that after school we bounded out the front door and hustled down Hamline Avenue to grab a city bus on Randolph Avenue or—to save money—we began hitchhiking. The STA guys walked out the front door and slid into Mom's waiting Cadillac.

Cretin didn't make bus transportation available when we were in school, and most of us had to figure out our own transportation. That usually meant riding a city bus, carpooling or hitchhiking.

Hitchhiking wasn't too bad except in the winter and in the rain, and it was relatively efficient because drivers like to pick up guys from Cretin. They liked to talk to us about the school and what we did there.

When you have a couple of hundred guys hitchhiking to school and back for four years, you're going to hear some stories. Consider:

Len Koehnen hitchhiked in from White Bear, along Lexington Avenue, and early on he got picked by a fellow in a 1948 Hudson Hornet painted flat black. The Goat Car.

As he settled into the front seat, he felt something nuzzle the back of his neck. What was that???? It was a goat! The driver had set up a plywood platform in the back seat so the goat could ride along. Len had a few more rides in the Hudson but never found out where the goats were headed or what they were used for.

"Well, okay," thinks Len. "A ride is a ride." But when he arrives at school and goes into his first period military inspection, he gets a surprise. When the inspecting officer comes to Len, he stops and stares. "What woman were you with this morning before you came in? Your uniform is full of hair." It was goat hair!

"I said, 'Sir, I believe it was a goat,'" says Len. Pause. "Don't say that too loud around here," the officer said, as he moved on.

After that, when Len would be thumbing and see the Hudson coming, he would duck into the gas station on the corner. "I wouldn't ride with him anymore." He was a nice guy, says Len, but the goats were too much.

An interesting sidelight to Len's Hornet is that Jay Leno, he of the Jay Leno's Garage vintage car collection, considers the Hornet one of the best handling American cars of the '50s. He has a perfectly restored 1953 green two-door Hudson in his collection in Burbank, Calif.

If you were in an after-school activity, you could be standing on the corner at 10:00 p.m. Some guys hitchhiking on the corner of Randolph and Snelling often would give up and take the bus if they had a dime for bus fare. "I often didn't have a dime," recalls one guy, "so we would drop a penny in the token machine and head for the back of the bus. The driver would watch us in the mirror, but he never kicked us off."

Pat McLaughlin recalls the time he rode with a guy who wanted to do more than just give a ride to a young Cadet.

"He talked about his girlfriend and then about her younger sister. And then he said, 'You and I should, you know...' and then as I'm getting close to where I'm going to get out of the car, he says, 'Are you as excited as I am?' Crazy. That's the first time I ever really hit anybody as hard as I could." **CHS**

Pranks and Urban Myths

Boys will be boys, they say, and pranks were not unusual at Cretin. Okay, maybe they were mostly silly time-wasters without any social significance. But we never walked out, we never protested in the streets—are you kidding?

If we would have been in the streets, The Brothers would have been right there with us, and they would have been watching the leaders with a tough eye. There were limits, after all, and we weren't going to go beyond them.

Still, there were student "uprisings" within the school.

There are many more stories than the ones we've documented here. Wonderful tales that sound like they might be true but that we couldn't verify. Urban Myths. Listen up.

Library "A Day." This one is true for sure. It was perhaps the biggest prank played during our tour. Librarian Adelaide pulled a book one day— *Teahouse of the August Moon*— because it mentioned geisha girls. Not fair, said some seniors, so a protest was organized.

The word was passed—take out a book or two and as soon as all the books are withdrawn from the library, return them all, at once. And so it happened. Adelaide, the librarian, was overwhelmed and almost had a nervous breakdown. Books were stacked everywhere.

The point was made, but I don't know if *Teahouse* was ever put back in circulation.

Company F, that rag-tag military group probably best known for its illegal white socks, scruffy uniforms, and out-of-step marching style, reportedly was pulled out of one annual Federal Inspection because officials didn't want the group to mess up the event.

"We were set up on the South Field, away from the inspection on the other side of the building, so no one would see us. We didn't have to march—because we really weren't capable of doing it," notes one member of the group."

Company F included several players from Tom Warner's baseball team, and it was only a matter of time until the Military and Warner collided. On one particular day, Company F was lined up in the parking lot across from the baseball field prior to a Cretin home game with De La Salle. As game time approached, Warner wanted his guys on the field. Not going to happen, said the Senior Army Instructor. No way.

Company F watched as Warner fumed and De La Salle waited. "We didn't know what to do." Finally, the De La Salle team got back on the bus and headed out. No game today. Cretin Forfeiture. Another notch in the belt of Company F.

Fort Snelling March. A similar ploy was used for another Federal Inspection, if we're to believe the stories we've heard. A group of non-performers, so the report goes, was assembled on the big day, and marched five miles to Fort Snelling and back during the inspection. "They didn't want us on the school grounds during the inspection," recalls one marcher.

Firecrackers. Did someone really light firecrackers in the gym during formation? The story is told enough times for one to believe there might be some thread of truth to the tale, although we could never put names to the act.

Stolen Rifles. Did a group of students actually steal a rifle and stash it in the locker of an unsuspecting Cadet? Stealing federal property was a felony offense, of course, and it caused a frantic school-wide search, led by the Military Department and The Brothers. The rifle was found, stashed in the locker of a very surprised student. No charges were filed, and no punishment inflicted.

Stolen Saltshakers. One day, all of the saltshakers disappeared from the cafeteria. It's not known who promoted this project or even why it was dreamed up. The saltshakers were found in a student locker and returned to the cafeteria. **CHS**

Senior Class Trip

If you don't remember anything about our Senior Class Trip, don't feel bad—only three guys participated—John Mueller, Mark Owen, and John Podvin. Just to refresh your memory—there was no official Senior Class Trip. These three guys just up and took off for California on their own one day in the fall of 1960, as winter approached.

Mueller cut his trip short and returned to Cretin, eventually rising to be a vice president with international responsibilities at 3M. Podvin and Owen have passed away.

Here's the trip story as we've been able to reconstruct it, arguably one of the most unusual events of our senior year.

Each of these three guys had a tough home life, and each was anxious to escape the coming Minnesota winter. Working for a rock band in California seemed like a really good idea at the time.

"It was probably the dumbest thing I ever did," recalls Mueller, "but we had what seemed like good reasons at the time. It was pretty stupid stuff, but we were full of p—- and vinegar and p——- off at everything around us, so off we went."

Mueller's family owned a 250-acre dairy farm, about 12 miles east of Hudson, Wis. "We raised every kind of animal known to man." John has lots of bad memories of the farm, especially the day as a youngster when he got chased by a big, angry goose.

As John recalls his situation, "I didn't like farming, and I knew I didn't want to live there. Anywhere but on the farm." He spent summers working on the farm and didn't like it one bit.

John spent the rest of the year in St. Paul, working two jobs to pay his tuition at Cretin. He set pins at the YMCA bowling alley on University Avenue and then bussed dishes at the Quality Cafeteria on Snelling Avenue. Between the two jobs, he paid his tuition in 10 months and then had a few bucks left over so he could go out on the town once in a while.

He was fast-tracking at Cretin, but hung out with Podvin and Owens, three loners who spent lots of time together. Check the '61 Yearbook, and you'll see that Mueller was "a top student" who "works arduously." Even though he worked two jobs, Mueller found time to participate in the Crack Drill Squad and the Science and Chess clubs and win an academic Merit Medal every year.

When they had the time and money, the three would go to the Wednesday night dances at the old Prom Ballroom on University Avenue, next to the Lexington Ballpark, where they listened to touring rock bands.

Do you remember the Prom? It was a popular spot for us to list to music and meet girls from the public schools. The Prom opened in 1941 and by the Fifties and Sixties it was a regular stop for leading Rock musicians.

Glenn Miller and Frank Sinatra appeared at the Prom, but during our Cretin years, stars like the Diamonds, Four Freshmen, Four Lads, Buddy Knox, the Everly Brothers, Conway Twitty, Bobby Darin, and Gene Vincent all performed there. The Beach Boys and Johnny Cash appeared after we graduated.

The Prom was a dance hall, not a concert hall, and it was THE place to dance with your date. Two thousand people could dance at one time on the 12,000 sq. ft. dance floor, and the Prom's super big stage could accommodate two bands.

You were able to get right up close to the talent, not see them from thousands of feet away like you do at venues such as US Bank Stadium.

A night at the Prom was affordable, too. Admission for a Buddy Holly concert January 28, 1959, that included the Big Bopper and Ritchie Valens, was $1.25; that's only about $12 in today's currency.

Gasoline was 31 cents a gallon at that time, and you could buy a pizza for 95 cents or half a fried chicken for $1.45 at the Highland restaurant on Ford Parkway.

A night at the Prom would only cost you about five bucks, including tickets, gasoline, and food. Can you believe that?

You may remember that a few days after Buddy Holly appeared at the Prom, on Tuesday, Feb. 3, 1959, he Ritchie Valens, and "The Big Bopper," J.P. Richardson were killed when their plane crashed in a farm field near Mason City, Iowa.

Was it any wonder that the Prom was a popular spot for Cretin guys and the girls we dated?

The Prom was demolished in 1987, and a new facility built in Oakdale.

John Podvin was especially into the bands and the musicians, and he worked to cultivate relationships with them. One artist he had ties with was a Black rocker who would become an international success—Little Richard.

Little Richard didn't appear at the Prom, but he made it big with his pounding piano and wild performances when he recorded his first big hit, *Tutti Fruitti*, in New Orleans in

September 1955. He followed that up with *Long Tall Sally*. Remember?

Given Podvin's love of music and his home life, it's probably not surprising that he could see himself making a career out of touring with the big bands as part of a support team.

What is perhaps surprising, though, is that he was able to talk Mueller and Owen into joining him. Maybe it was the magic hours at the Prom that had something to do with it.

The three teenagers would meet regularly at the Ran-Ham or the Nook or the Malt Shop, three burger joints across the street from Cretin, to share tales of their unhappy homelife.

As the Minnesota winter closed in during the Fall of 1960, their talk turned to sunny California. Could they head to the Coast and hook up with bands as support workers? Podvin thought so, and he talked the others into the idea. Soon, the dream became a reality.

" I don't know how it came up, exactly, but eventually we decided to head for California and join the bands," recalls Mueller.

During one gripe session they agreed to meet at the Greyhound bus depot in Downtown St. Paul and take off for California.

On the day they departed, "We had about a hundred bucks among the three of us," says Mueller. 'It was really stupid." When they got to the bus station, they found out the first bus south was headed for Fort Dodge, Iowa. "It was late October, early November, and we really just wanted to get out of Minnesota. So, off we went."

The next stop was Omaha, and by that time, the guys had spent their cash.

"We usually stayed at YMCA's," recalls Mueller, "but I remember we stayed in a hostel for kids in Omaha. And, of course, by that time we were pretty much out of money, so we had to look for work." They ended up washing dishes in small restaurants and cleaning floors, taking low buck jobs to pick up a few dollars.

They didn't have enough money to buy bus tickets, so they had to hitchhike out of Omaha, thumbing separately because no one would pick up three teenagers. They aimed for a town with a YMCA where they would connect, work for a day, and then hit the road again. "It was interesting but pretty stupid," says Mueller.

Mueller met a lot of weird characters while hitchhiking but had only one bad experience. "I got picked up south of Omaha by a guy who was obviously gay, and he wanted to have a little fun with me. I decided I didn't need that, so, I just had him pull over and I got out.

"There weren't as many nasty characters as there are today. Sometimes, it took a little longer, but we got where we were going. Those were interesting times."

The group's original intent, long before reality set in, was to hook up with bands. "We had these aspirations of supporting a rock group in California. But, frankly, I never got there." Podvin and Owen made it to California, but their job hunt didn't work out and the pair eventually returned to St. Paul, although under dramatically different circumstances than did Mueller.

"I got to Memphis," remembers Mueller, "and I could see this was going nowhere; it was just a dead end. We were going to be worse off than we were here, struggling with the home life. In Memphis, we got jobs in the YMCA, we were basically janitors for the place. I said, 'This is nuts.' Things might have been bad at home, but it's not as bad as this is going to be. We had nothing. So, I got back on Greyhound and came back home."

Mueller arrived before Christmas—he was only gone about a month—and was readmitted to Cretin. He graduated with the Class of '61 and built a successful 40-year career at 3M where he rose to vice president with global responsibilities.

Podvin and Owen went on to California, returning to St. Paul several months later after struggling to find work with bands but they were not readmitted to Cretin. Podvin graduated from Johnson High School and Owen from Monroe. Mueller recalls that his return to St. Paul wasn't pleasant. "For a couple of weeks, it was pretty tough going."

He made peace with his family and then went back and met with the Brothers at Cretin. "I thought they were going to kick me out, but I had pretty good grades, so they said, 'You're going to have to do some penance, but we'll let you back in.'"

Mueller had to plead his case before a team of Brothers, and he was sweating it. "I was afraid to look anyone in the eye. I had good grades and I think that's what saved me." He was assigned to perform janitorial duties for Brother Wilfrid, the assistant principal. This wasn't too bad because Brother was a known heavy smoker, and the pair took smoke breaks outside, in back of the cafeteria.

Brother Wilfrid was a nice guy and wasn't the only one who smoothed the road for Mueller. "Brother Eugene took me under his wing, and he helped me get through it. He was the only one I could talk to, and I remember seeing him once or twice a week. He would say, 'Don't worry about this, you'll get through this. Just bite our lip and shut up.' Four months into it, I was fine."

Mueller remembers Brother K. Mark as "an inspiration. He was so smart. He really was an inspiration to me."

Mueller was back in class full-time at Cretin after Christmas vacation. "I was a hulluva lot wiser than when I was going out. I did some stupid stuff after that, but it never equaled that trip."

The three eventually created substantial careers for themselves. Owen became an air traffic controller in Texas, and Podvin dedicated himself as a chemical dependency counselor. He was a strong supporter of AA.

Even while working two jobs, Mueller posted an impressive record at Cretin. He was a member of the Crack Drill Squad and the Science Club, among several other activities.

He was a member of the National Honor Society and was awarded full academic scholarships from St. Mary's College and the College of St. Thomas.

Mueller took a job as a lab technician at 3M in Maplewood after he graduated from Cretin. Fortunately, 3M had a substantial education reimbursement program, and Mueller took full advantage of the benefit.

Using his background in chemistry, he enrolled in the pre-med course at the University of Minnesota until it came time to cut up a cadaver.

"This one had been worked on before," recalls Mueller, "and it didn't look good. I thought, 'No way is this for me.' He dropped the pre-med program right then and there, switching to chemistry.

Mueller eventually earned degrees in Chemistry and Mathematics from the University of Minnesota and an MBA from the London Business School while working his way up to vice president at 3M. He held top management positions for 3M in South America, Japan, and Europe before retiring in 1998.

In his current retirement, Mueller enjoys global investing and travel.

Memories of Cretin? "I remember the ethics and serenity of the Christian Brothers," he says.

Senior Class Trip? Definitely. Memorable? Without a doubt. Repeatable? Not so much. **CHS**

Discipline

Not all my Cretin memories are pleasant, especially the one concerning the day I got whacked in the face by Brother L. Mark for talking in a Quiet Zone.

On this day, Brother Mark was leading a group of us through the tunnel between two buildings, the old original structure, and the new addition. No talking here because the sound echoed in the concrete tunnel. I was walking near Bro. Mark when there was talk somewhere in the back. I turned, to look for the troublemakers, and as I turned back, I never saw the punch coming from Brother Mark.

His powerful right hand caught me in the face—and it began to puff up immediately and it stayed swollen and discolored for several days. The worst thing about this whole experience is that I was innocent— one of the few times I was on the straight and narrow!

That's one of the interesting things about The Brothers: they treated you like a man and they didn't hesitate to use the muscle.

One husky football player—a rough, tough guy who pushed 230 lbs. and was known to batter opposing linemen— squared off after school one day with slim Brother Francis and it wasn't a pretty sight. Brother was a former boxer, and the event was over in two punches.

Prof. Jim Adams was in charge of our advisory room, Advisory 205. He was a friendly, easy going guy, who didn't push the discipline angle much. But one day he was absent, replaced by a new Christian Brother.

Brother Francis was a small guy with blond hair, and he just stood in front of the room and quietly watched us as we bumped and jumped through our early morning hijinks. New Brother. We had this guy, no problem. Most of us were bigger than he was. We would show him how things worked.

Then he slowly, deliberately rolled up the flowing sleeves on his hassock, showing us his forearms. Big, strong forearms. Really impressive for a little guy. They seemed to carry neon signs that flashed, DANGER. DO NOT ENGAGE.

Oh, damn. Could be bad, we thought, as we moved quietly to our desks. The advisory period was over before any of us could get hurt. Nothing had to be said. Message received.

We were prohibited from spinning the tops on trash cans because it made so much noise. One day, a freshman disregarded the rule and Bro. Josephus caught him in the act. Brother had huge forearms developed as a weightlifter and was known—and feared—for his strength. He picked up the offending freshman by the shirt with one hand and deposited him on top of the lockers. When last seen, the young man looked very puzzled as he tried to figure how to get down from his perch. **CHS**

Military

Cretin's mandatory Junior Reserve Officer Training Corps. (JROTC) unit was one of the oldest units in the country, and it was one of the largest during our four-year term. In 1960, Cretin's all-male student population was 1,150 pupils., making it possibly the largest such unit in the country, according to military sources.

At Cretin's founding in 1871, the curriculum included mandatory military training based on that used in military institutes; Cretin was one of the first high schools to take this approach. Following the National Defense Act of 1916, which created the Reserve Officers Training Corps (ROTC), Cretin began its full JROTC program in February 1918. Cretin was formally certified in the JROTC program in February 1919, one of the first high school JROTC programs in the country.

Every year there would be a federal inspection to determine if the JROTC unit measured up to national standards. If it did, it would receive "Honors With Distinction." Cretin never missed receiving this honor, and no class wanted to be the one that broke the string of excellent ratings.

The mandatory JROTC requirement was dropped by the school in 1984.

"We are certainly within the top 10 oldest program in the country," says Sgt. Major (Retired) David Berrisford, who serves at Cretin. "No question about it. Quite frankly, in the Junior ROTC world, if you were to mention Cretin, people would recognize the name as having been in JROTC a long, long time."

Shattuck Military Academy, founded in Faribault in 1858, also was an early proponent of JROTC, also beginning its program in 1919. St. Thomas Academy, Mendota Heights, opened in 1885 and in 2015 it dropped its JROTC program.

JROTC is designed to "instill in students the value of citizenship, service to the United States, and personal responsibility." Most JROTC instructors are retired or reserve officers and enlisted noncommissioned officers. The four-year curriculum at Cretin included topics such as leadership, ethics, history, marksmanship, and close-order drill.

Initially, all instructor salaries were paid by the Army, a nice benefit for Cretin because it could add faculty at no cost. Some instructors also taught regular classes, such as geometry and math. Subsequently, that contract was rewritten, and salaries now are split between the school and the Department of Defense, still a nice financial benefit for Cretin. Funding also is provided for uniforms, training materials, and other operating expenses for mandatory.

The normal tour of duty at Cretin for an instructor is three years, but some stay much longer. Master Sergeant Larry Smith (Ret) served at Cretin for 24 years (1984-2008) and LTC Ret. Steven Dahlgren served for 18 years, from 1992-2010.

The military program involved annual federal certification inspections, to ensure that the program was up to standard. This meant shining the brass belt buckle and lapel

emblems. What to use for the job? Brasso brand liquid pol-
ish, of course, in the red, blue and silver can. You can still
buy the "Easy To Use" stuff at Amazon in an 8 oz can for
$2.98. Brasso's 8,265 Amazon reviews are positive and gen-
erally have a historical twist. "I used it on my belt buckle
and buttons when I was in the service and decided to give it
another try and it works as well as ever," wrote one reviewer.
Many Cretin guys still have a can of Brasso at home.

Cretin was unusual, if not unique, in its setup as a military institute in 1960. Most military high schools across the
country were expensive boarding schools where students
often were sent for disciplinary reasons.

One former Cadet who wrote about his time at Linton
Hall Military School in Bristow, VA, said students were sent
there because they required discipline, because parents were
looking for a babysitter or because students needed to learn
English. None of those reasons applied at Cretin. **CHS**

Instructors

Many of the military instructors who taught us at Cretin were extraordinary soldiers on active duty assignments, deserving of our highest respect, even though most of us often didn't treat them that way.

"I did not realize how fortunate I was to be taught by Korean War combat Army sergeants in our military classes," says Mike Wold. "I remember two of them to this day – Sergeant McIver and Sergeant Cole. They were both examples of good military discipline and leadership."

Sgt. First Class John Bell (1960-1964) was killed in action in Vietnam and Master Sgt. Robert E. Cole was awarded two of America's highest military honors for outstanding battlefield service in Korea during which he was wounded several times.

"The military guys were really supportive of me," says Greg Poferl, Cretin Class 1965. "I valued the memory of Sgt. John Bell. We really loved the guy. After I enlisted, I was at Ft. Leonard Wood, and I heard that Sgt. Bell had been killed in Vietnam. I just sat there and thought, 'How can that be possible?' He was like our hero. We didn't see him going into combat. But he did and he was killed. It just registered that he was a good guy, he wanted us to be of good character; and he was more like a friend to a lot of us. He was able to build a relationship with us."

Master Sergeant Robert E. Cole (1958-1962) was awarded the Distinguished Service Cross and the Silver Star, the second and third highest U.S. Army military honors after the Medal of Honor. Sgt Cole was given the awards for "extraordinary heroism" in military operations against an armed enemy while serving in Korea. Here's what a portion of Sgt. Cole's citation noted:

> *"Master Sergeant Cole distinguished himself by extraordinary heroism in action against enemy aggressor forces near Sinsan-ni, Korea, on Sept. 2, 1950. On this date, a section of Sergeant Cole's platoon was (providing support) in an attack on well-fortified enemy positions.*
>
> *"When the advance faltered due to an enemy counterattack, Sergeant Cole made his way through intense enemy small-arms, mortar and automatic-weapons fire to reorganize the dispersed elements of his section.*
>
> *"As the intensity of the attack increased, he crawled to the one remaining machine gun, removed the dead gunner and began pouring a deadly hail of fire into the ranks of the attacking enemy.*
>
> *"Although twice wounded by enemy grenade fragments, Sergeant Cole refused to be evacuated and continued to deliver effective fire upon the enemy."*
>
> *"When his ammunition was exhausted, Sgt. Cole withdrew, dragging his machine-gun with him. While organizing the few remaining elements of his section in preparation for a counterattack, he was ordered to the aid station for medical treatment.*
>
> *"When the high ground was retaken, 18 enemy dead were found in the vicinity where Sgt. Cole's machine-gun was mounted."*

Thank you for your extraordinary service, Sgt. Cole.

Sgt. First Class Willis McIver was perhaps the most colorful of our military instructors, and anecdotes about him abound. "In my opinion, without question, the most memorable and insightful teacher was Sgt. McIver," says Mark Robertson. "He taught us as much about life as about military science."

One time Sgt. McIver caught Len Koehnen wearing a chest full of ribbons he had purchased at the Army/Navy surplus store in downtown Minneapolis to wear in one of the big parades. "Congratulations on your service in Guadalcanal and Iwo Jima, Koehnen," McIver said when he saw the display. "You've got two seconds to get rid of those ribbons!"

Another time, he dragged a Cadet to the military office for disrespecting Sgt. Cole. McIver related the Korea incident and Sgt. Cole's citation, and then asked, "And what have you done, you sonofabitch?" Nothing. "I was really embarrassed," said the Cadet. "I was just glad to sneak out of that office."

Jim Davis didn't want to wear his uniform, so he told Sgt. McIver that it irritated an incision from a recent surgery. McIver wasn't buying it. "Davis, if you don't wear that uniform tomorrow, you'll have my size 9 1/2 boot up your ass." Next day, and every day, Davis was in uniform.

Following a lecture describing different types of ammunition and their uses, McIver told the class about a soldier who tried to avoid combat by shooting himself in the foot. Foolishly, he used an armor piercing round that went right through his foot, instead of an anti-personnel round that would have given him a serious wound. Medics patched him up and sent him back into action. Lesson: use the right ammunition for the job.

Another day, Sgt. McIver instructed the class on the use of the .45 automatic pistol. McIver's description: "the maximum effective range of this weapon is stated as 50 yards... because that's about the maximum a guy in good shape can throw it."

Also serving as military instructors during our time at Cretin were:

- Major Charles J. Hoyt
- MSG Kenneth Jackson (1955-1959)
- MSG Ralph Deyo (1955-1957)
- MSG Ambrose Bean (1956-1959)
- MSG James Hardy (1956)
- MSG John Daily (1956-1957)
- MSG Lyle E. Warner (1957-1959)
- MSG Grant Jones (1960-1962)
- MSG James Cullen (1961-1962)
- SFC James Davis (1960)

Thank you for your service, gentlemen. **CHS**

Military Activities

When you have 249 teenage boys spending four years dealing with career non-coms in a mandatory military atmosphere, you're bound to produce unexpected activities. Consider these reports from our class and some others:

Many students had only one pair of black military shoes, so they had to be treated with care. Mike Wold:

> *"I remember before one of the inspections, I took my black shoes to the shoe repair shop to be fixed. When I came back to pick them up the day before the inspection, the store was closed. I only had three pairs of shoes—my black dress shoes, my tennis shoes and a pair of yellow moccasins.*
>
> *"I decided to wear my yellow moccasins for class the next day. I stood in line in the morning and the sergeant was so rushed that he did not look at my shoes and gave me a pass for the day.*
>
> *"During the parade that day, I marched by the reviewing stand wearing my bright yellow moccasins. After we passed in review, one of the student officers ran up to me to gig me for wearing the moccasins, but I just pulled out my official pass signed by the sergeant— he could not believe it."*

Many of us wore so-called Ike Jackets, short, heavy woolen jackets designed after the jacket worn by Gen. Dwight Eisenhower in WWII. Most of us didn't have raincoats, and we never carried an umbrella. "When several of us were on a bus," recalls Bill Kuhns, "the smell of the wet, warm, wool could be amazing... I can still smell it now...a bit like a 'dead mice in a wall' smell."

Officer uniforms and gear were not cheap, especially the sabers and the black leather Sam Brown belt used to holster the saber. Today, a saber costs about $250 and the belt costs $125. Because of the cost, often Cadets shared the equipment, which was no easy task when both men participated in the same inspection.

I'm certain this happened more than once, but here's one story. One Cadet, whose family didn't have a lot of extra cash because it was sending five kids to Catholic high schools, couldn't afford the Sam Brown belt, but it did have a saber passed down from a previous generation. That's a start. Now, his buddy had the belt, so they shared resources. The process worked just fine, since they were in different classes.

Not so good, however, during the annual inspection. Solution: Since the guys were inspected at different times, they faked fainting spells and headed for the restroom where they swapped gear. It worked.

Speaking of sabers, this wasn't something that a lot of guys were used to wearing—it wasn't a normal thing to salute with a saber, you know? Well, during one of the first inspections a new officer was preparing to salute the inspecting lieutenant colonel in charge of the Cretin regiment. As the colonel stepped in front of the Cadet, the Cadet whipped out his saber and nearly knocked off the colonel's hat.

"I'm turning all shades of red, and the guys in back of me in my platoon were struggling not to laugh and the colonel was trying to adjust his hat with as much dignity as he could muster before moving on."

The sabers could really cause problems for the unskilled. At the Military Ball, during the Grand March, the officers formed an elegant and dramatic archway with their sabers for the top officers and the debutants. The March went just fine, until the officers had to replace their sabers in their scabbards. Our hero stuffed his in backwards and got it stuck halfway down. He spent the rest of the evening with his saber sticking up out of the scabbard and answering embarrassing questions from his friends.

Long hair was not permitted by the Military—hair could only reach the top of the ear and the collar in the back. But long hair was a sign of manhood in the Sixties, so Cretin guys stuffed their long hair up into their hat during inspections.

At one inspection, several guys got caught for long hair and were sent off to the Military Office for a "haircut." The Cadets had to trim each other's hair with a pair of 12" shears—it wasn't pleasant. "We really did a job on each other," recalls one, "and we were the laughingstock around school 'till the hair grew out, which was several weeks."

The military classes involved regular written tests, of course, just like any other class. We soon learned that the same test was used in every class throughout the day. The first class had to work at it, but every other class had the questions, so the tests were no problem.

Until the instructors unfairly changed the tests and caused real problems for every other class throughout the day before we caught on to their deception. **CHS**

Crack Drill Squad

The Traditions of the Cretin Crack Drill Squad go back at least as far as the 1939-'40 school year when the team won the Pershing Military Drill Competition on Jan. 28, 1940. Cretin's team beat teams from St. Thomas, St. Paul Academy and the University of Minnesota.

The 1960-1961 senior 10-man edition of Cretin's Crack Drill Squad under the direction of Commander Paul Ossmann represented the best that Cretin's military program had to offer. It was the showcase team the school used when it wanted to demonstrate its Military expertise to the public.

There were two 10-man platoons: the Freshman/Sophomore platoon commanded by James Lethert, and the Junior/Senior platoon, commanded by Paul.

The team usually performed five or six times each year, but arguably its most prominent performance was the day it spent participating in the St. Paul Winter Carnival Grande Day Parade.

Members recall the 1961 Parade on Jan. 28, 1961, as a cold day, and well they should. Temperatures were near zero with winds gusting to 25 mph down the Parade route on Cedar Street and through downtown to the St. Paul Auditorium. The *Pioneer Press* newspaper reports of the parade noted that 16 women were treated for frostbite and at least one woman was hospitalized because of the cold.

In the staging area while preparing for the parade, the guys were already cold, so they hunted up the biggest float with the brightest lights they could find, and they used the lights as heaters, crowding around the big lights as they tried to keep their hands warm.

"We had to wear white gloves as part of the uniform," recalls Bill Kuhns, who was in the squad all four years. "But we added several extra pairs for the Carnival."

They wore long underwear too, of course, and they simplified the routines so they could maneuver in the cold without fumbling the rifles.

It was so damn cold," remembers Jay Laramy, "that I thought for sure someone would drop a rifle, but nobody ever did."

The cold was even worse, because of the frequent stops made by the parade, and the long route kept the guys from ever warming up.

The Team's tough practice schedule during the year helped it to work through the cold, though. The Squad practiced several days each week during the summer and continued to practice two or three days a week for an hour before school.

"The guys were pretty focused by the time we got to a performance," says Laramy.

Ossmann even remembers one squad member who had to spend the summer in Europe with his parents, who promised to practice routines while he was away. "I didn't think he would be able to keep up when he returned," says Ossmann, "but he didn't miss a beat. Apparently, he really had been practicing by himself during the summer."

The Squad used the slim, well balanced Springfield 30.06 rifles that had special decorative plating on the receiver and bolt instead of the bulky M1 models. The Springfield models spun much better. "We didn't have them silver plated," says Kuhns, because most of the blue collar families didn't have money for that sort of thing.

The rest of the Crack Drill uniform embellishments to our standard military uniform consisted of a while helmet, white neck gaiter and white spats. Very impressive.

In addition to the Winter Carnival, the Squad's other performances were usually at smaller, special functions and at girls' high schools. One noteworthy event for the '61 Squad was the trip to Villa Maria Academy, about an hour's drive south down Hwy. 52, near Frontenac, Minn.

Villa Maria Academy for Girls was an elegant high school boarding facility located on 124 acres that opened in 1891 and closed in 1969, following a disastrous fire.

Cretin boys participated in several dances each year at Villa Maria, but none were as successful as those featuring the Crack Drill Squad. In most cases, the guys would stand on one side of the room and the girls on the other. The thing that made it most uncomfortable was that the girls were pretty smooth and sophisticated and we boys, were, well, a bit rough around the edges, and clumsy. Many of the girls were Big City Ladies from Chicago or foreign countries, and we thought they were going to eat us alive.

The Crack Drill Squad, on the other hand, came across as pretty sophisticated, and were treated very well. Bill Kuhns: "We were treated like visiting dignitaries. We were just treated beautifully by everyone. It was like they were in awe of us and in awe of the uniforms. I have really positive memories of that evening. I don't remember feeling like a bumpkin, but maybe I was so much a bumpkin I didn't even know it."

The team performed at most of the other girls' schools with similar results, from the reports that we have.

The long hours of practice meant that there were few, if any, mis-steps during the performances. One episode does stand out for Jerry Filla, class president. It was during the Squad's performance at the Class '61 Commencement in the St. Paul Auditorium. When he banged his rifle butt on the concrete floor, the wood split, and he had to perform the rest of the routine with his rifle virtually hanging in pieces. **CDH**

Rifle Range

Every Cadet during our time at Cretin was required to pass a marksmanship test on the basement rifle range once during his four years. That meant scoring at least 40 points on a target that is 12 inches high and 10 inches wide with a 10 point bullseye in 10 shots from 50 feet with a .22 rifle.

Three positions were required, prone, kneeling and standing. The actual target circle is only 1.75 inches in diameter.

The range in the school basement isn't very big—28 feet wide and 70 feet long. There are eight shooting positions, so eight guys could shoot at the same time.

Today, the Cadets no longer use a .22 caliber rifle as we did because it's considered too dangerous. Instead, they use a .17mm Crossman air rifle. It's safer and the Cadets still receive rifle training. The .22 rifles at Cretin were Harrington and Richardson, Model-12 .22 caliber.

As you might expect, these exercises did not always go quite as smoothly as planned.

One Cadet, who was not experienced with guns, was dismayed to see that when he reviewed his target, it was pristine—unmarked by bullet holes. He had completely missed the target on all of his 10 shots!!!

"Crap (or something similar to that)," he thought. But no problem. Being a creative sort, he dug out a pencil and punched 10 holes in the paper target, enough to give him a passing score. Success!

Given the lack of expertise by shooters on the range, it wasn't surprising to find that some targets contained more than 10 bullet holes.

One gunner remembers that there was a metal sign located off to one side of the range, situated at a 90 degree angle to the firing range. It was not anywhere near the target area.

Somewhat surprisingly, when the shooting began, there were frequent "ping, ping, pings," of bullets ricocheting off the sign. Remember, this sign was at a right angle to the range. Shooters were missing down range by 90 degrees!

The good news is, to our knowledge, no one in our class was ever wounded, even with our limited skill sets and lack of attention.

As an example of our expertise with weapons, we even were able to put together two rifle teams, commanded by Lawrence Lindberg and Greg Kline. Sgt. First Class John Bell was the moderator. **CHS**

Christian Brothers

During our time, Cretin was run by the Catholic order of the Christian Brothers, also known as the De La Salle Brothers, or simply the Christian Brothers. In 1960, there were 28 Brothers at Cretin and 18 lay teachers, but The Brothers ran the show. Without a doubt.

In my experience, the Christian Brothers believed that a slap in the head was an important tool in the educational portfolio for teachers of young men, and I saw this tool applied liberally during my time at Cretin.

A Long Road

The Christian Brothers trace their beginnings to 1679 when John Baptist De La Salle began teaching poor boys in Reims, France. Three years later, the first teachers decided to call themselves "Brothers," when they opened their first school.

Jump ahead to 1851 when Bishop Joseph Cretin opened a school for boys in St. Paul, Minnesota. Twenty years after that, in 1871, the Christian Brothers came north from

Chicago to teach the boys at Bishop Cretin's school. Today, The Brothers teach more than a million students worldwide.

In 1889, the first Cretin High School for boys was opened in St. Paul, and in 1928 the present building at Hamline and Randolph avenues was opened. The Brothers' residence is physically part of the school, connected to it by an all-weather breezeway. The residence was originally built in 1927 for 20 Brothers, and in 1954, an additional 13 bedrooms were added, enough for 35 Brothers.

During our time at Cretin, the Brothers lived at the facility and ran the operation 24/7. They weren't employees, they were more like mentors, like parents. They didn't go home at 3:00, and they didn't have family problems. Cretin was their life, and the students were their focus.

The Brothers were innovators. In 1937, they set up the Cretin Students' Credit Loan Association as a source of funding for students who did not have the cash to pay tuition and expenses. Was this America's first student loan program? The organization was phased out when the need for this funding declined.

A FIRM HAND. A HELPING HAND

Firm discipline, man-to-man, was a teaching rule of The Brothers. One '61 classmate put it this way: "Even when they disciplined you, it always felt like they weren't doing it to hurt you, they were doing it to help you, you know. They wanted you to be better than you thought you could be. Maybe it's because they didn't have any family to take care of."

There were constant high expectations. You were expected to be a man, you were expected to be better tomorrow than today. The Brothers weren't intolerant, but they didn't let you get by. Good enough? No, that's not good enough. "You're going to have to do better. And tomorrow, make sure that you are better." That seemed to be The Brothers' Rule.

At Cretin, The Brothers told us we were the best, and that we should always remember that and apply it to whatever we did. We still carry that thought: We're the best.

Although there were several lay teachers at Cretin, The Brothers were the driving force at the school—and we use the term "force" intentionally. They provided mentorship and training in the classroom and on the athletic fields with directness and a firm hand, one that often held a stiff rod. Their presence provided a unique aspect to the Cretin Culture.

There was no other combination of Christian Brothers-U.S. Army leadership and all-male discipline operating in Minnesota during our time, or few places in America. It was unique and memorable and effective.

The Brothers working at Cretin devoted their life every day to building boys into responsible young men and winning athletes, even though this task, in some cases, seemed to be nearly impossible.

Here are some of those men who were especially influential in that daily battle of our development. **CHS**

Brother K. Mark
(Jack Lane)

Brother K. Mark was my English teacher at Cretin, and he helped me learn to be a writer. But I didn't know it at the time.

I was a teenager, and I didn't know who I was or what I could do, or would do, and I wasn't smart enough to accept his guidance. It took me decades to learn the lessons he was trying to teach me during those years.

I still have a folder of papers I wrote for him 65 years ago. I marvel today at the messages he sent me on those red ink splashed papers, and my total lack of recognition of them or acceptance of them.

"Someday, soon," he wrote on one paper, "you'll be a very good writer." I still remember that comment 65 years later, but I did not accept that critical direction at the time.

Brother K. Mark had a major impact on many people; his effect on our class was substantial, more so than any other teacher or coach we had. He received more positive comments from members of the Class of '61 than any other faculty member during our surveys, group discussions, and interviews.

"I shall never forget him," says Dennis Herzog. "He was an inspiration to us all."

He focused on the leaders in the class and impacted them, and that influence spread throughout the class. His English classes were stiff. With him, there was a certain standard that you better meet, and you did meet it. He didn't beat you up without propping you up when he got done with you. There was a ray of sunshine when he finished with you. But he wasn't around a lot—you didn't see him at dances or even in the halls. He worked behind the scenes.

Brother K. Mark had a quietly firm way of handing out discipline. Mal Scanlan was an important cog in Cretin's hockey team and on the day of one game, he had a run-in with Brother K. Mark, which he lost. Mal's assignment was to memorize a short poem, but Scanlan decided not to do it. No reason, just, not going to do it. Brother told him to return at 3:00, after school, and recite the poem. Nope, not going to do it. Oh, oh. We're getting into dangerous territory, here.

Brother gave him several more chances, every 30 minutes, until it was time for Scanlan to leave for the hockey game. You know how that turned out. Not happening. Scanlan's parents were in the stands to see him play, and when he didn't show up, his trouble got worse.

"When my parents came home from the game," says Scanlan, "I had to tell them why I wasn't at the game. To paraphrase my Dad, 'Memorize the poem by 7:00 tomorrow morning because that's when you and I are going to see Brother Mark.' And that's what we did. I recited the poem for Brother. I didn't try anything like that again. End of lesson. End of story."

Len Koehnen says it took him many years to get over his anger with Brother Mark. "To embarrass me and push me,

Brother Mark made me read my report card to the class and then sit in the front row. My card was finely tuned for maximum fun and minimum grades. I was underperforming, and it wasn't until I was 50 that I realized how much he helped me."

Brother K. Mark, under his birth name, Jack Lane, earned a PhD in educational administration from UW Madison after leaving Cretin, moved to Chicago, his hometown, settled in at DePaul University, and married. He was a generally gifted fellow, athletically, artistically (wonderful baritone/tenor voice), and intellectually. He served as godfather to a number of children of his former students from Cretin.

Dr. Jack Lane headed up the operation now called the Office of Mission and Values at DePaul. Seems perfect. Eventually, a scholarship at the school was named after him, the John J. Pedicone, Sr. and Dr. Jack Lane Scholarship.

Brother K. Mark was with us only our first three years, but he quietly had a major influence on many of us, perhaps more so than any other adult at the school. He was an inspiration to us all.

Cretin '61 and Brother K. Mark. You can't separate the two—they're one entity, and we're all so much the better for it.

When he left Cretin in 1960, Brother K. Mark moved to Lansing Catholic High School in Lansing, Mich., as principal. Not surprisingly, several Cretin graduates taught there with him, Dick Herron and Bill Treacy, among them

Next, Brother Mark took the reins at St. Mel's in Chicago.

We reached out to Jack when researching this book, but health considerations prevented him from talking with us. **CHS**

Brother K. Thomas
(G. Thomas McCarver)
1934-2014

Brother Thomas was an impressive presence in the classroom and on the athletic field, where he coached football.
He was a strong and gifted athlete, skills that we tended to
overlook in the religious men.

One day, at football practice, a punting challenge was
laid down. Coach Len Horyza was a known power kicker,
and some of the boys thought they were pretty good, too.

Brother Thomas joined in, but he was just an assistant
coach and a CB, not to be considered a real challenger.
Game on.

As it turned out, Brother Thomas's booming kicks were
well out of range of the other efforts, even those from Coach
Horyza. Big surprise!

Another day, Mal Scanlan remembers promoting the
skills of Dick Strutz, Cretin '59, the outstanding baseball
catcher. Strutz played football at Nebraska and minor
league baseball.

"I was telling Brother Thomas that Strutz was the best catcher anywhere," recalls Scanlan. "Not better than my brother," says Brother Thomas. "Not even close," responded Scanlan.

Turns out, Scanlan was wrong. Tim McCarver, Brother Thomas's brother, was a major league Hall of Fame catcher for the St. Louis Cardinals National League baseball team!

"To this day," says Scanlan, "I remind Strutz that I promoted him against a Hall of Fame catcher!"

Brother Thomas spent two years at Cretin before eventually leaving the order. Brother Thomas was born in Memphis and died in St. Paul at age 80 in 2014.

Mention Brother Thomas to many former Cretin athletes and the response is often puzzlement—"I can't imagine why an athlete like him would join the Christian Brothers." It's still a mystery to us. **CHS**

Brother Jerome Francis

(Thomas Jerome Rademacher)
1936-2012

Brother Jerome Francis saved the eyesight of John Crenshaw when John was splashed in the face with a bottle of
nitric acid during a chemistry lab experiment. Brother
Francis grabbed John, pushed his head under a nearby fau-
cet, and washed out his eyes and face before there was any
lasting damage.

Don Wolkerstorfer has fond memories of Brother Francis: "When I was a junior at Cretin, he picked me to be his
lab assistant for his chemistry class. It was the beginnings of
a relationship that continued long after high school. In fact,
I would see him every few years, and this continued until he
passed away. He will always be an inspiration to me.

"Events I really enjoyed while working at Los Alamos
National Laboratory were the visits from Brother Jerome
and some of his students from St. Mary's University in
Winona. Every year, Brother Jerome would take about 10

science students to a 'big science' lab over spring break. Such labs included Argonne National Laboratory, Oak Ridge National Laboratory, and Los Alamos National Laboratory. Every four years or so he would come with his students to Los Alamos. When he did, I would host them and set up tours of Laboratory facilities."

Brother Francis was born in Minneapolis, Minn., entered the Juniorate in 1951, and the Novitiate in 1954, in Glencoe, Missouri. Entered De La Salle High School in Minneapolis, attending one semester before entering the Juniorate. In 1955, he enrolled at St. Mary's College in Winona and earned his BA in 1958. He began teaching at Cretin that year and stayed for three years.

He died Feb. 15, 2012, in Winona, and is buried in St. Mary's Cemetery in Winona. **CHS**

Brother Josiah Pius
(Arnold Kurtz)
1889-1985

Brother Pius sat by the Cafeteria door and acted as the Cafeteria monitor while we were at Cretin. The term "monitor" probably is too strong—Brother Pius was more of a pleasant greeter. When we think about Brother Pius, we remember the free lunches that came with Cafeteria duty—for the workers and for their friends. Brother Pius was only 71 when he guided the food operation, but to us, at that time, he seemed truly ancient. It seemed as though he was at Cretin forever.

Brother Pius was born in Chicago and attended De La Salle High School there before entering the Novitiate in 1906 in Glencoe, MO. He taught at Cathedral High School in Duluth, Heffron High School in Rochester, Minn., and Cretin, plus several other schools in Illinois, Tennessee, and Missouri.

Brother Pius was an avid bird watcher, and he formed the first Audubon Bird Club in the Twin Cities area. He moved to the Little Sisters of the Poor in St. Paul and died there Nov. 11, 1985, at age 96, after having spent 79 years as a De La Salle Christian Brother. He is buried in Resurrection Cemetery, Mendota Heights, MN. **CHS**

Brother Kevin
(Bartley Vincent Mackey)
1915-2008

Brother Kevin was one of the most respected Brothers at Cretin, where he spent many years in administration. Later, he served as administrator at several schools in Chicago. He was assigned to Cretin in 1952 and served as assistant principal and principal until 1962. He returned to the classroom at St. Mel's High School in Chicago and was named principal at De La Salle Institute in Chicago in 1965.

Brother Kevin was a no-nonsense leader, but he was a man who was very approachable. Despite his duties as principal, Brother Kevin still had time—and a genuine interest—in serving as team bus driver and mechanic. He always had us say the rosary on our way to football games, but we never prayed coming back after we won. (Were we only praying for victory?)

He received his BA from St. Mary's College in Winona and began teaching in 1937. Three years later, he moved to Boy's Town in Nebraska for four years. Prior to moving to Cretin in 1952, he earned his MA at St. Louis University while teaching in Kansas City. After leaving Cretin, he taught and served in administrative posts in Illinois and Michigan before retiring in 1980 from Driscoll Catholic High School in Addison, IL, where he died at age 93. He had been a De La Salle Christian Brother for 75 years. **CHS**

Brother Ladislaus Mark LaMont
(Victor Giles LaMont)
1913-2004

Brother L. Mark, known to have a powerful right hand, twice was assigned to Cretin, most recently in 1958-1960 when he served as Assistant Principal. Born in Duluth, Brother Mark spent much of his career working and teaching in the Twin Cities.

He entered the Novitiate at Glencoe, MO, in 1931 and graduated from St. Mary's in Winona with a degree in English in 1935. Following graduation, he taught religion, English and mathematics at De La Salle High School in Minneapolis for one year before moving to St. Mel's High School in Chicago.

From 1936 until his retirement from Grace High School in Fridley in 1978, Brother Mark taught and served in administration at more than 15 assignments from Amarillo, TX, to Illinois and to Iowa and Minnesota.

When he retired, Brother Mark remained in Fridley to become a volunteer at St. William's parish, before continuing his volunteer activities in St. Paul's Highland Park and the Frogtown community. In 1993, he moved to the Cretin-Derham Hall community where he lived until his death.

He died at age 90 on Feb. 2, 2004, in St. Paul, and his cremated remains were interred at Resurrection Cemetery in St. Paul. He had been a Christian Brother for 73 years. **CHS**

Brother Kiaran Wilfrid
(John Weil)
1914-1975

Brother K. Wilfrid was known by many as the Uniform Czar because he distributed the military uniforms every year. He was a bit casual in his fitting process, and it wasn't unusual for him to measure you for pants with a waist of 34" but give you a size 38." "Take what you get." He was a heavy smoker and a Coca-Cola phenom. He was assistant principal at Cretin, and also seemed to be the "Dean of Discipline," especially when it came to laying down the rules for smoking and general conduct.

Cretin had a No Smoking rule, but stories abound about Cadets sharing a smoke break with Brother Wilfrid. Ask John Mueller—who skipped school for about two months in 1960 to take a "Senior Class Trip"—about working off his penalty performing janitorial work for Brother Wilfrid. This assignment wasn't too bad because Brother was a known heavy smoker, and the pair took smoke breaks outside, in back of the cafeteria.

Another story is told about Brother Wilfrid lecturing the baseball team about their conduct and rough language in the dugout during a tournament in St. Cloud. As he was wrapping up his lecture, Jim Clarkin ran off the field, ranting loudly about a bad call with a long string of, let us say, ungentlemanly language. Brother Wilfrid stomped out of the dugout and wasn't seen again for the rest of the tournament.

Brother Wilfrid attended Christian Brothers College High School in St. Louis as a Cadet. He completed his undergraduate degree at St. Mary's College, Winona, in 1937. His career as a business teacher and his lifetime as an avid sports fan took him to De La Salle High School in Minneapolis in 1937; St. Mel's High School in Chicago, 1938-1949; Cretin, 1954-1961; and Christian Brothers High School in St. Louis in 1961-1975. He served as a sub-director three times at Cretin and twice at CBC in St. Louis.

He was born was born Nov. 14, 1914, and near St. Louis, MO., and entered the Novitiate in 1933 in Glencoe, MO. He died of a stroke Nov. 13, 1975, in Clayton, MO., at the age of 61 and is buried in Calvary Cemetery in Glencoe, Missouri. **CHS**

Brother Lorian Josephus
(Raymond Carl Wilhelm)
1922-2011

Brother L. Josephus was known as "Muscles," behind his back, of course, because he was so darn strong. Reportedly, he was a boxer and lifted weights, but no one challenged him on either of those counts.

One time, so the story goes, he almost was challenged on the football field. He was getting his B Squad ready for a game the next day when Varsity football Coach Tom Warner called for the team to run plays against the Varsity at the other end of the field. No Dice, says Brother Josephus, we've got work to do.

After the second rejection, Warner ran down to the B Squad practice area and faced them across one of the field's yard lines. "If you want to play on the Varsity next year, get moving." Brother Josephus' response was immediate and direct. "I'll drop the first one who steps across that line."

What a dilemma. Nobody moved and Warner returned to his Varsity business without a scout team to run plays.

Brother Josephus spent only four years at Cretin with our class, but he made a strong impression. He used to help set up the boards for the outdoor hockey rink, and players still talk about how he would single-handedly carry boards into position, a process that normally required two or three players.

He ran a tight ship. Three checks in his black book in class and you were headed down to the basement for a triple-treatment with his cut-down hockey goalie stick.

Tim St. Martin, one of the hockey team's goalies, remembers one time he was downstairs receiving whacks with the stick, when he recognized the weapon. "Hey, Brother, that's my hockey stick," he wailed. Unfortunately, for Tim, he didn't get a reprieve.

Brother Josephus was born in Covington, KY, and graduated from Newport Catholic High School in 1943. He then entered the Novitiate and became a De La Salle Christian Brother, a life he led for 69 years.

He earned a BSS degree in 1946 from St. Mary's College in Winona. His first teaching assignment was at St. Mel's High School in Chicago, where he remained until 1950.

At St. Mel's, he taught history and religion and began a lifelong devotion to the sports department of every school where he was assigned. At St. Mel's, he served as Athletic Director, but devoted most of this extracurricular time to coaching baseball and wrestling.

In 1950, Brother Josephus was assigned to Cretin, where he spent seven years before being transferred in 1957. He returned to Cretin in 1958 and stayed there until 1963.

In 1963, he returned to his alma mater, Newport Catholic High School, where he was a busy guy. During his 14 years there, he taught Latin, religion and history and coached three sports.

After leaving Newport in 1977, Brother Josephus taught and coached at five high schools in Kentucky, Tennessee, Ohio, and New Mexico until he retired in 1986. Brother Josephus died Sept. 6, 2011, in Ft. Thomas, KY. **CHS**

Brother Eugene
(Eugene P. Gaffney)
1930-2012

Brother Eugene taught English and served as the moderator for the 1961 Cretinite Yearbook.

John Mueller, one of the guys who took off on an unauthorized Senior Class Trip, remembers Brother Eugene very well. When John returned to Cretin, Brother Eugene "took me under his wing," John says, "and he helped me during my return to school. He was the only guy that I could really talk to, but I remember seeing him at least once a week, maybe twice (a week) and he would say, 'Don't worry about this, you'll get through this. Just bite your lip and shut up.' And four months into it, I was just fine."

Brother Eugene resided in Apple Valley, Minn., after leaving the Christian Brothers order. Even in his retirement, he continued to educate, teaching English as a second language.

He raised two daughters and was grandfather to five grandchildren. **CHS**

Brother Richard
(Richard Shrake)
1922-2011

Great basketball player from Winona. Coached B Squad basketball. Quiet guy but called me out in basketball practice for loafing. I remember, to paraphrase his comment: "Delmont, speed it up. You have the misguided notion that you appear like a Shining Beacon and that the ball will always come to you. You're not a Shining Beacon." **CHS**

Brother Gabriel
1922-2011

Brother Gabriel was remembered by several classmates for his kindness. Brother Gabriel called on John Lamey one day in Latin class for an answer that he couldn't immediately deliver. "Nobody home," said Brother and moved on to the next student.

"I also remember his Latin classes," says Don Wolkerstorfer. "I think we spent more time learning about life than Latin. Often, he would come into the class and say, 'Men use your time wisely, I am up to here (with work, raising his hands).' Every Friday we would have to translate the gospel for the following Sunday.

"I found this very useful, since the Mass was still celebrated in Latin. Several of us took four years of Latin. We had Brother Gabriel until the second semester of the fourth year. Then we had a new Latin teacher, fresh out of school. He realized how little Latin we knew. But then I think he realized this was our last semester and backed off. I learned a lot from Brother Gabriel in addition to the Latin."

Bill Kuhns had similar memories of Brother Gabriel, but also remembered that the religion class he was in usually was required to memorize the next Sunday's Gospel. "For those who could memorize well, that was a boon... memorize the English Gospel for one class, then 'sight translate' the Latin gospel into English for another. Even those of us who were lousy memorizers usually recalled enough to get by."

Brother Gabriel used the term "men" when addressing us as a group. As in "OK, men, clear the decks for action..." He was a highly effective, gentle, but powerful, man.

Bill remembers, most, Brother Gabriel's caring, almost beatific, smile and visage... he seemed to care, deeply, about every one of us. As, of course, did most faculty and staff there. **CHS**

Lay Faculty

The Christian Brothers ran Cretin and set the tone in philosophy and discipline, but the Lay Faculty made a huge contribution as well.

Aside from the coaches who also served in the classroom, men such as Tom Warner, Ted Joyce, and Len Horyza, science teacher Prof. Hank Conroy may have had the highest profile among the non-coaching lay teachers at Cretin.

Prof. Hank Conroy taught Physics and Chemistry and ran Advisory 113. While he was proven to be a very good teacher, he also was known for his ability to rattle heads and bust bodies. He was rumored to have had experience in the boxing ring before he moved into the classroom.

Prof. Conroy was known for his food-stained ties, rumpled appearance and grouchy attitude. In the classroom, he was known for his demanding requirement for neat workbooks. If your workbook was messy, you were dead. Hand in a clean workbook, and you had a great chance to pass his class.

Here's how Pat McLaughlin managed his passing grade. Looking at his book, Pat knew he didn't have a chance of passing, but he also knew that his buddy, Bill Treacy, was tracking for a good grade because of his super workbook. Solution? Just hand in Treacy's workbook as Pat's project.

"I took the two books," says McLaughlin, "and I unwound the spiral bindings on each one and just switched covers." Voila! Pat had a new book. Now, just get Prof. Conroy's sign-off, and he was home free. But to do that, he had to go to Conroy's house on a Saturday morning, after the last day of school.

"I was terrified. His wife answered the door, unsmiling, and said, 'He's in the basement.' The house looked just like Conroy himself and his classroom—a little bit disheveled." Pat headed down the narrow dark basement stairs to Prof. Conroy's workshop, cluttered with coffee cups and cigarette butts.

"I was so fearful, going down there. The guy's going to just absolutely (kill) me. So, I went down there, and I gave him the thing and he just looked at me—he didn't say a word. 'All right.' And he signed off on it. I got to walk out of there, and I made a novena a couple of times after that. I was never so frightened in my life."

As the guys recall, Bill received a low mark for the class "because of all the times I had p_____ off Hank during the year." Pat, on the other hand, says, "I think Hank gave me a high mark because he was stunned that I had done ANY work at all in his class."

Two covers, one book, two grades and two happy Cadets.

It turns out that Prof. Conroy actually was a pretty nice guy—and smart, too—outside of the classroom. Len Koehnen remembers working at Honeywell as an engineer when he was asked to meet a new guy the company was about to hire. It was Prof. Conroy!!!! "I was shocked. But, as it turned out, we worked side-by-side for three years and I had a great time with him." Things are never as they seem.

Was Prof. Conroy a good teacher? It seems as though he was a very good teacher. Just ask John O'Reilly. In December 2021 John was riding a bus in Cairo, Egypt, when some passengers were trying to convert the temperature from Celsius to Fahrenheit. John immediately knew the answer was 77F, using Conroy's formula of 5F-9C=160. It works! I mean, really. John remembered Conroy's chemistry formula after 60 years?

Prof. McKeown taught bookkeeping, and he must have done a great job because at least two of his students from our class became accountants and got their CPA rating. Rich Peacha admits he didn't do very well in most classes, but he loved Prof. McKeown's bookkeeping lessons. "One of my proudest moments at Cretin was attending his bookkeeping class." Rich earned straight A's and learned a lot. Went to biz school after Cretin and became an accountant for life. Ended up owning his own auditing firm. "Not sure what path I would have taken in life without Prof. McKeowen," Rich says.

Dan Rask says Prof. McKeown introduced him to his life's work as an accountant. "I'm exceedingly thankful to him."

Joe Patton, taught algebra and geometry... and St. Thomas College football history, circa 1922. He's remembered for three things: his geometry, his college football and his painful yardstick known as the Board of Education.

Tom Warner, coached football and baseball, and taught biology and physiology classes. Dr. Gary Francis, the internationally known cardiologist, says that it was in Warner's class that he first became interested in biology and the way the human body functions. Thanks, Tom, for your contribution to medical science.

Ted Joyce, coached football and hockey, and taught social studies; his afternoon sessions offered a needed respite in an often stressful day for Cretin students. "Ted provided a wonderful afternoon break after we suffered through a lot of tough classes and punishment early in the day," says one of his students.

Don't get the wrong idea—Ted wasn't a pushover. As a former quarterback, he had a deadly passing arm and would hit an inattentive student in the back of the classroom with a well-thrown hockey puck or eraser. "It really hurt when he hit you in the head with a puck."

Len Horyza, football and basketball coach, also taught geometry for 35 years. The former Marine was known for his unique forms of discipline such as forcing you to hold books out in front of you. See how you like that after 10 or 15 minutes.

Len also had his patented "Index finger-board" exercise. Try this: stand close to a wall and then lean on the wall, touching it with your two index fingers. Slowly, back up until you're leaning at about a 30 degree angle. How long can you last? **CHS**

Athletics

Sunday, Oct. 16, 1960, dawned bright and clear as more than 10,000 avid Twin Cities high school football fans prepared for the afternoon battle of high school unbeatens between Cretin and Benilde High School at O'Shaughnessy Stadium in St. Paul.

Cretin was riding a 29-game winning string and was eyeing its fourth consecutive Central Catholic Conference championship. The young Benilde team from Hopkins included a number of St. Paul area players and was looking to establish its reputation.

The tough fight—featuring stunning long runs by Cretin halfback Dick Harren and a heartbreaking Cretin goal line fumble—ended in a 13-13 tie, breaking Cretin's winning streak, and leaving the huge crowd in stunned silence as it drifted toward the gates.

The game was the highlight of an athletic season at Cretin that featured gut-wrenching near misses in football, hockey and baseball.

In honor of the four-season undefeated record from 1957, 1958, 1959, and 1960, the football teams were inducted into the Cretin-Derham Hall Athletic Hall of Fame in June 2022.

TOP STUDENT-ATHLETES

There was no official recruitment program at Cretin but attracting top student-athletes was not a problem during our time. Dedicated alumni watched for good athletes and directed them to Cretin as did the network of coaches at the local Catholic grade schools.

Our class featured many accomplished, champion-level, multiple-sport athletes. It wasn't unusual for guys to swap their football pads for hockey gear and then their hockey sticks for baseball bats.

Cadets such as Harren, Scanlan, Stewart, Hoffman, Clarkin, St. Martin, Enestvedt, Droubie, Haugh, Haigh, Smoliak, Daulton, Busch, Komives, and Lievers led the way. Today, you don't see many guys playing more than one sport, and certainly not at a championship level.

These top athletes maintained a good attitude and a respectful relationship toward their non-athletic classmates; they didn't brag about their exploits. "You couldn't be cocky," recalls one of this group, "or you would be ripped to shreds."

Brothers often hooked up with good basketball players after a local grade school game or tournament to discuss their high school plans. "You really couldn't turn down Brother's invitation," says one ex-player.

Of course, the Sisters at the Archdiocese's network of Catholic grade schools were active recruiters, too. It seemed as though there was only one high school option for the best student-athletes in their eyes: Cretin. The Citadel on the Hill. And they pushed it.

Considering that there were some 600 eighth grade boys in the area taking The Entrance Exam for about 200 spots in the next class at Cretin, it's not surprising that the school boasted a robust athletic program.

Cretin was in a fortunate position because it drew the best student-athletes from all the Catholic grade schools in the St. Paul area. In 1960, Cretin was the Number One Catholic high school draw from about 25,000 pupils in nearly 45 St. Paul area Catholic grade schools that included St. Luke's (1,400), St. Mark's (1,500), Nativity (1,000), St. Pascal (900), St. Columba (1000), Sacred Heart (950), Presentation (1,100), St. Francis (600), St. Casmir (600), Holy Spirit (700), St. Joseph's West St. Paul (1,000), St. Michael's West St. Paul (600), St. Matthew's (1,000), etc.

By comparison, in 2021, the number of local grade schools had dropped to about 25 and the student population to slightly more than 7,000. St. Mark's was gone, St. Matthews was gone, and St. Joseph's in West St. Paul dropped from 1,000 to less than 400.

Cretin also was fortunate to work with very talented and dedicated grade school coaches who prepared the best athletes to work and play ball at Cretin. Guys like Joe Meyers at St. Mark's, Bob Doane at Nativity, John Friedmann at St. Luke's, and Jim Pacholl at St. Francis, to name just a few. Joe Meyers was a true legend in Twin Cities athletic circles—for about 36 years, he served as athletic director and coached several sports at St. Mark's, with its huge pupil population, located only three miles from Cretin.

Sixty years after we graduated, Cretin's robust athletic feeder system was gone.

While Cretin produced lots of great athletes, including many who played at the highest professional levels, in the NFL, NHL, NBA, and MLB, the coaches stand out for us. Tom Warner. Ted Joyce. Len Horyza. Brother Thomas. You don't forget guys—mentors—like these men.

Cretin posted 29 straight victories in football, before the tie with Benilde. Then we closed out the season with three more victories, giving us an unbeaten string of 33 straight games over four years. We never lost a football game while in high school. Not many can say that!! That's why those four football teams (1957, 1958, 1959, 1960) are now in the Cretin-Derham Hall Athletic Hall of Fame.

Tom Warner's mantra seemed to be: "I want that play run, and I want it run, right. Run the off tackle play, and this is the way it's supposed to go. And if it doesn't go like this, we're gonna run a lap or we're gonna come back and we're going to do it again. And we're going to do it 'till we do it right."

Quarterback Mal Scanlan talking about our football practices: "I thought it was great preparation. We knew where we were going and where they (the opponents) were going to be. And if they went where they were supposed to go, they didn't have a f_ _ _ _ _ _ chance." It's very true that we always knew where to be.

WINNERS

During our senior year, Cretin finished at the top in football, hockey and baseball, and produced an excellent record and several award-winners in basketball.

Here's our Championship Run, that was so close to perfection:

- **Football**, Co-champion, Central Catholic Conference, undefeated but we had the 13-13 tie with Benilde;
- **Hockey**, lost 13th annual Minnesota Prep School Invitational championship 2-1 to SPA after defeating them 5-1 in the regular season. Cretin did win the CCC hockey title with a 12-0 record;
- **Baseball**, lost 1-0 and 9-6 to St. Cloud Cathedral in the championship round of Central Catholic Conference tournament at St. Cloud.

- **Basketball**, finished fourth in the state tournament after losing in the second round to champion De La Salle, 42-36.

The football team was undefeated for four years; the only blemish was that 13-13 tie with Benilde. We played that game without our starting half back Jim Stewart, who broke his arm in the Fargo-Shanley game.

It's interesting to compare our 1960 football operation with that of the 2021-2022 Minnesota 6-AAAAAA Champion, Lakeville South, that finished the season at 13-0.

Lakeville South had a student population of about 1,800 in 2021 and Lakeville North, located only two miles away, also had an enrollment of about 1,800 pupils. Cretin had an enrollment of 1,200 in 2021.

The Minnesota High School League classifies schools by size for competitive purposes. The highest classification for football is 6-AAAAAA for schools with enrollment of 1752 and above. Next is 5-AAAAA for schools with enrollment of 1047-1751.

Cretin football had always competed in 6-AAAAAA but in 2021 it dropped back to 5-AAAAA—it just couldn't run with schools that had 50% larger enrollment pools from which to draw, especially when it's feeder system had dried up. Today, Cretin has a smaller enrollment than many schools and it has a feeder system that is only about 25% as large as it was in 1960.

Physically, the Lakeville South team was nearly twice as big as the 1960-61 Cretin team; it had 82 lettermen, compared to our team of 44 guys. The Lakeville front line was much bigger than our Cretin guys, too. Our starting offensive line averaged less than 200 pounds: Joe Delmont (170), Mark Hoffman (165), Bob Komives (178), Tom Haugh (190), Chuck Reischel (181), and Bob Busch (191) and Nick Christensen (174).

Cretin's offensive line in 1960, totaled 1,245 pounds, and averaged 177 pounds. Our heaviest guy was Bob Busch, at 191, and Mark Hoffman was the lightest at 165 pounds.

The offensive line at Lakeville South totaled 1,605 pounds, and averaged 230, with the heaviest going 280, and the lightest being 205, about 15 pounds more than our biggest guy!

We had four football coaches, Tom Warner, Ted Joyce, Len Horyza, and Len Mrachek. Lakeville South had 13, including a Cornerbacks coach, a Defensive Backs coach, a Culture coach, an Outside Linebackers coach, a trainer, Offensive and Defensive Line coaches, and Offensive and Defensive coordinators. The sophomore team had another nine coaches.

Coaches

Tom Warner (Coach, Mr. Warner). Ted Joyce (Thumper). Len Horyza. Bill Tierney. Ted and Len were quiet leaders, Warner was a volcano. Ted coached hockey and assisted Warner with football and baseball. Horyza assisted with football and coached basketball. Tierney coached basketball.

Tom Warner. Warner won titles in football and baseball while at Cretin, but he was also a remarkable biology teacher. All of the coaches at Cretin had to teach classes as well as guiding teams on the field. Len Horyza was considered by many as a solid math teacher and Warner—surprisingly—was given high grades for his classroom performance as a biology teacher.

Gary Francis, who is a highly respected international cardiologist, says Warner was the teacher who most got him interested in biology and medicine, a startling statement to some of us.

Dr. Francis is Professor Emeritus of Medicine at the University of Minnesota and a cardiologist who specializes in congestive heart failure. He has published more than 560 scientific papers and has edited or co-edited 23 books. His work has been cited more than 50,000 times in the scientific literature, placing him in the top one percent of all scientists internationally.

Despite the accolades he received as a teacher, Tom's main claim to fame was as the football coach who led Cretin to four undefeated championships in four seasons.

Warner grabbed several honors for his coaching achievements. He was named national Coach of the Year in 1960 by the New World Catholic Press. One voter from the *St. Paul Pioneer Press* newspaper had this to say about Warner: "(He's) a tremendous coach. He has a powerful offense and brilliant defensive strategy; but most important of all, he knows how to handle young men and to instill confidence and desire in them. His great record in the toughest Catholic league in the state is undeniable proof of his ability."

Warner said at the time that the powerful Cretin offense was very simple: "We have very few plays. And they are relatively simple. But we try to learn the ones we do have to perfection." Warner shared his success with Joyce and Horyza: "They deserve a world of credit. They're the best."

Warner also coached four years as the assistant coach for the South team in the annual North-South All Star game. The South won four times during Warner's tour, evening the series at 4-4.

Warner took over as head coach for football and baseball in 1956, after coaching at Marshal Central Catholic. The players referred to him as Coach Warner, but it could have been "Vulcano," given the way he regularly exploded on the field.

Warner, who went on to become athletic director and coach football at Butler University, died shortly after making the move. Coach Warner died of an apparent heart attack at age 48. He just blew up. Much too soon.

Coach was a graduate of Minneapolis De La Salle High School and a 1951 graduate of the University of Minnesota. He served as vice president of the National Association of College Baseball Coaches.

Ted Joyce. Ted graduated from Cretin in 1946 and had baseball tryouts with the Dodgers and Cardinals before heading to St. John's College where he played football and hockey. He graduated in 1952 and enrolled at the University of Minnesota where he was doing graduate work until a near-fatal car accident forced him to drop his studies in April.

He began coaching hockey at Cretin in September that year. In his remarkable career, Ted's teams won 10 titles in the 12-year history of the Minnesota State Private School Invitational Hockey Tournament and finished second in the 1961 tournament. His longest winning string was 28 during the 1954 and 1955 seasons. Ted's winning attitude carried over to football where he helped coach the team to 33 wins without a loss in four years.

Ted wanted to play the best, so he took his hockey team to International Falls to play two games against the International Falls High School Broncos. Cretin split the two games, being one of the few Twin Cities teams to win at the Falls.

"It's a shame they (Cretin) can't be in the state tournament," Larry Ross, coach of the Broncos, said at the time.

One of Ted's claims to fame in the classroom was his art of keeping order in the back of the classroom by tossing erasers and hockey pucks at the disrupters. Ted was a former quarterback and he usually hit what he aimed at.

Getting hit with an eraser was embarrassing but hockey pucks were a different story. "It hurt to get hit in the head with a puck," says one of Ted's targets.

Ted was popular, though. "Ted was a safe port in a stormy sea," recalls one athlete who had Ted for an afternoon social studies class. "It was a relief to go to Ted's quiet class in the afternoon after being beaten up all day. He did have a very accurate arm, (when throwing hockey pucks) though."

Len Horyza. Len was another winner. He taught and coached at Cretin for 35 years, winning two Class AA boys basketball state championships in 1991 and 1993 and finishing second in 1992. Before coming to Cretin, he taught and coached at Ashland (Wis.) High School for five years.

Len coached B Squad football for many years. "We told Lenny to teach our football players how to win, and that's what he did," said football coach and athletic director Rich Kallok.

Even though he could be very tough, Len was very sensitive, too. His wife, Betty, suffered with Alzheimer's disease for nearly a decade when Len died.

Pat Reusse wrote about the situation in the *Minneapolis StarTribune*. "Len took his wife everywhere with him—to the Cretin-Derham Hall games...and to dinner at their favorite St. Paul restaurants a couple nights per week.

"A lot of people might not leave the house in such a situation. Lenny was just the opposite. He made what would have been a sad situation for most people into a comfortable situation."

Horyza was a star athlete in football, baseball, basketball and boxing at Superior (Wis.) Cathedral and the University of St. Thomas, where he is a member of the Hall of Fame. He's also a member of the Minnesota High School Coaches Hall of Fame.

Horyza was a nice guy, but he wasn't one to be pushed around. He was a Golden Gloves boxing champion and spent two years in the Marine Corps.

There's a story about a Cadet who yelled down the hall at Horyza as he was leaving for summer vacation: "Bye Lenny." Horyza let it go. Until the next September, when he caught the kid in the hall on one of the first days back, and slapped him in the head, with a succinct, "It's Mr. Horyza to you."

The action was dually noted by the student body.

Horyza died of an apparent heart attack July 15, 1995, at the young age of 62.

Dennis Denning, the award-winning coach and athletic director at Cretin, recalled Horyza: "He was enjoyable, and really funny, as a teacher and a coach."

Horyza's funeral was held at Holy Spirit church, across the parking lot from the Cretin football field and gym, the scenes of so many of Len's successes.

"I don't know where that funeral could be held to be big enough for all the people," Denning told the *St. Paul Pioneer Press*.

Cretin coaches never let us get too cocky. Football coach Tom Warner was one of the most intense people I have ever met. Really frightening for a high school kid. We feared him more than any opponent.

He was a great motivational speaker. One speech before a St. Thomas game when we were seniors was especially memorable.

"This is your last chance to beat these guys and you better take advantage of it."

What?

"These guys own the companies where you're going to be working and you'll never be able to say another thing to them. You'll never get a raise from them. This is your last chance to @%# them."

There was no way the Cadets were going to beat us after that speech!! We thrashed them 27-6.

Warner had several rules. One was, "No ice cream during football season." I love ice cream, but I wasn't about to get caught by Coach Warner. No way.

I had my share of putdowns on the football field from these coaches.

One game against SPA, I made what I thought was a great, leaping catch on a pass from Scanlan. I had to leave my feet, stretch out horizontally and grab it on my fingertips. Very nice. Ask Dick Haigh—he was running a pass route in the same area.

After every game, there was a dance at the school, and we all wore our letter jackets and talked about the victory. I, of course, was talking about my catch, and I asked Mr. Horyza, how he liked the grab.

"Perhaps if you would have run the (pass) route properly, you could have made a routine catch," he said dryly and walked away. End of catch talk.

LESSON: Don't brag yourself up. Let your accomplishments speak for themselves.

I had one other tough experience with Horyza. One day, at practice, he was throwing passes to the receivers. "Len," as we called him behind his back, was a big, strong guy. Anyway, we were running fly patterns—run straight down the sideline from the line of scrimmage as far and as fast as you can go—and he would hit you. I ran my pattern way down field, looked back for the ball, and shoot he hadn't even thrown it. What's the point? He can't throw it this far. So I eased off the gas. And watched as the ball sailed about a mile over my head.

As I jogged back to the group, a bit embarrassed, he asked why I stopped running. What was I supposed to say? That I underestimated him? No way.

Any way, he said maybe I needed practice running. "Hit the track." He made me run the cinder track until the end of practice. I was exhausted. Believe me, that was the last time I eased off on one of Horyza's passing drills.

Ted had his hockey pucks, of course, and Horyza had two tricks that kept us in line. One punishment involved standing with your arms extended out in front of you while holding a book in each hand. Try that for a few minutes.

Another little gimmick that Len had was this: Stand a few feet from the wall, and lean against the wall, putting all of your weight on your two index fingers. That's all the support you had. You can't last long doing that.

Listen to what it was like to play ball at Cretin, from Jim Stewart. Jim was a small guy from Grand Forks, North Dakota, who starred in football, hockey and baseball at Cretin, winning All-State honors in hockey.

DIVISION I AND BEYOND

Several members of Cretin 61 played sports in Division I and beyond. For example:

- Tommy Haugh played three years of hockey at Providence College before playing several years for the U.S. National Hockey Team and national hockey teams in Sweden and Japan. Tom was a national celebrity in Sweden for his hockey exploits while playing for Sweden.

- Dick Haigh and Mal Scanlan played hockey at Providence College. Dick transferred to the University of Minnesota where he played hockey before playing for the U.S. National Team in 1967 and 1968. He followed up his playing days with a long career as a collegiate hockey referee in the WCHA (Western Collegiate Hockey Association).

- Scanlan transferred from Providence to St. Thomas College in St. Paul where he played hockey. He had a successful football coaching career in high school and college.

- Tim St. Martin also played goalie in semi-prof Canadian teams, and in Europe for the US Army.

- Dick Harren was a scholarship player and a football starter before suffering a knee injury at the University

of Minnesota. Had 177 yards against Wisconsin before being rolled out of bounds and injured his knee.
- Mark Hoffman played football at the University of Minnesota. He lined up against Bobbie Bell and Carl Eller in practice, but that didn't work out too well.
- Gary Droubie played first base for the 1964 University of Minnesota baseball team when it won the Big Ten Championship and the U.S. College World Series
- Charlie Reischel lettered in football at Harvard.
- Bob Komives lettered in football at Dartmouth.
- Many others played in MIAC.

There were many outstanding individual athletic performers in our class. Here are just two examples.

Dick Harren may have been the best all-around athlete in our class, starring in football and putting out solid performances in basketball and baseball. He even won an event in a track meet at Cretin while playing a baseball game, running the 100 in about 10.4 seconds. Warner wanted to show off Dick's speed, so he sent him to run the 100 in his baseball uniform while he had a few minutes during the baseball game. Crazy.

Dick played football, basketball and baseball for three years at Cretin, but his career was plagued by knee injuries. He injured his left knee as a junior in the Shanley game and it slowed him down for the rest of the season. He returned to lead the team's offense in his senior year.

While making the All-American team as a senior, Dick drew lots of attention from big time college scouts. He got a long look from Notre Dame, but eventually lost out because of his bad knee. Instead, he took a full academic scholarship to the University of Minnesota, where he played football. But he caught more bad luck there and injured his right knee. He rehabilitated the knee and played several Big Ten games. But he pulled a hamstring in the Wisconsin game and never played again.

Tommy Haugh. Arguably one of the most successful post-high school athletes in our class was Tommy Haugh, who starred for international hockey teams in Sweden and Japan as a goaltender. He was most successful playing for Rogie BK, the Swedish professional team, in 1965-1967 and 1967-68. He also played for the Tokyo, Japan, Seibu Bears in 1968-69.

Tom, with his booming personality and hockey exploits, became a national celebrity in Sweden.

After graduating from Cretin, Tom played two years for Providence College and two years for Team USA in the International League in 1963-65.

Tommy, as we called him, was a stocky guy and one of the heaviest players on the football team, weighing in at close to 200 lbs. But he was a gifted athlete, a quick and smart goalie, and a smooth tennis player.

"Tommy was such a smart and astute goalie," says Jim Stewart, "and that's probably why he went so far. He was a student of the game. He looked for every advantage he could get.

"Tim St. Martin was a very gifted goalie, too, and to have two of them on the same team... They probably were two of the top four goalies in the state at the time we played. No question about it."

Tom also was a talented musician, fingering his way across the piano keyboard or the strings of a guitar or banjo. He could move into a bar, sit at the piano and in moments be leading a bar-wide songfest. "He was an unbelievably talented entertainer," notes one of his followers.

In fact, Tommy, who never had much money, had to hitchhike to Providence, traveled the world several times, playing hockey and working the streets with his music to pay his way home.

Another tough competitor at Cretin was Tim St. Martin, who split goalie time with Tom for four years. As coach Ted Joyce said, "It's too bad you two guys came through at the same time."

Tim played in Canada and later in Europe for several years while he was in the Army. He remembers one day being shocked out of a sound sleep on the base in Europe when Tom burst into the barracks and screamed in his high pitched strident voice, "Get your ass out of that bed, St. Martin."

To this day, St. Martin has no idea how Tom wangled his way onto the U.S. Army base. Nobody is surprised when they hear this story.

AWARDS

As an aside, the 1959-60 season was a banner year for Cretin. Coach Tom Warner was named national Catholic Coach of the Year, and senior end Dick "Red" Warren (Cretin Class of '60) and junior guard Mark Hoffman were named to the national All American team.

Cretin placed seven men on the 1960 All State team. In addition to being named to the All-State team, Dick Harren also was the leading scorer in the CCC. He was All State Honorable Mention as a sophomore but then was injured in his junior year. Chuck Reischel and Mark Hoffman were named as guards on the team, and Bob Komives manned the center spot. Harren also was named to the All-America First Team, and Reischel was named to the All-America Second Team.

On defense, Cretin added Mal Scanlan, Bob Busch and Tim St. Martin to the All-State team.

Cretin's dominance wasn't appreciated by many teams and one time some disgruntled competitors ripped up the hedge spelling out Cretin's name on the north side of the school. Several Cretin players waited the next night to catch them in the act, but they never showed again.

"We knew it couldn't be the cake eaters from St. Thomas," said one player, "because they weren't strong enough to rip out the bushes." **CHS**

Game Reports
1960-61

8-0-1
Co-Champions
Central Catholic Conference

At the beginning of the football season, we circled three **BIG** games: Fargo Shanley, Benilde, and St. Thomas Academy. The biggest game of the year—in fact, the biggest game of our four years—was the Benilde game at O'Shaughnessy Stadium, Sunday, CCC. The 13-13 tie maintained our undefeated record, but it broke our record of consecutive wins. Bummer.

Still, we were co-champions of the Central Catholic Conference, the fourth consecutive year we grabbed that title.

The standing room only crowd of 10,103—considered a record for a Minnesota high school football game at that time—was stunned by the outcome. Dead silence as we filed out of the stadium.

Dick Nesbitt, a local TV sportscaster, said the silence was something he had never heard before in his broadcasting or professional football career.

Dick Harren posted our 13 points running for two dramatic touchdowns and kicking the extra point. Joe Delmont saved the tie by blocking the extra point try by Benilde's Skip Olshefsky.

Unfortunately, we played without our starting halfback, Jim Stewart, who had broken his arm in the Fargo Shanley game.

Fargo Shanley. Another big game was against Fargo Shanley, the North Dakota champions. We beat up Shanley on a dark, rainy day at the old Midway Stadium, 39-6, in front of 2,500 people. It was the back end of a home-and-home series with the North Dakota powerhouse. We beat them in Fargo 13-7 in 1959, Shanley's only loss in three years at that time.

The game started badly, and it looked as though a major upset was in the making when Shanley scored an early touchdown on a fumble recovery and led 6-0 late in the first quarter. Then, with 2:22 remaining in the period, Mal Scanlan returned an intercepted pass 55 yards for a touchdown, and we were on the way to our 27th straight victory in four years.

Stewart led the way with a touchdown in the first half and an 80-yard kick-off return for a TD to open the second half. He didn't play much the rest of the game, but still ran for about 50 yards against the North Dakota guys. He broke his arm in the third quarter and had to sit out the next two games. We missed Stewart's offensive punch when we played Benilde three weeks later.

Scanlan added two more touchdowns late in the game on short yardage plunges.

There was never a dull moment dealing with the coaches. Scanlan remembered he was playing practically every down in that game—offense, defense, kick-off, and kick-off return. It was the fourth quarter, we had just scored, he was dragging, and Warner called for the kick-off team. Scanlan asked for relief. 'Get somebody else, Coach. I'm tired,' Warner went ballistic: "Tired? You're a quitter, Scanlan, a quitter. Get your a_ _ out there." Scanlan trudged back onto the field.

Benilde. The Cretin-Benilde game was the match-up of the year for players and fans alike, and more than 10,100 fans jammed O'Shaughnessy stadium for the battle of the unbeatens. Cretin trailed twice and had to battle back to force a tie and keep its unbeaten string intact at 30 games.

Benilde jumped to an early lead in the first minute of play: Cretin fumbled the kick-off and Benilde recovered on the Cretin 39. Facing a fourth down and five yards to go, Benilde hit a 34 yard touchdown pass to Steve Berg. The Berg TD was especially frustrating since Berg graduated from St. Mark's Grade School, a major feeder school for Cretin located only 10 minutes away!

Benilde's point-after kick hit the crossbar and dropped across for the point. Lucky.

Cretin retaliated moments later, when halfback Dick Harren took a handoff from Mal Scanlan on the Cretin 20, bounced over left tackle and outraced Benilde defenders for an 80 yard touchdown. Harren's point-after kick was blocked, leaving the score 7-6 with 6:18 to go in the first quarter.

Cretin had several chances to score before the half but couldn't push it across the goal line. Charlie Reischel blocked a Benilde punt and Cretin got the ball on the Benilde 40. Harren picked up 35 yards on a sweep around right end. First and goal from the 5-yard line. Two plays picked up two yards before a fumble was recovered by Benilde on the one-yard line.

Cretin had one more chance on the last play of the first half when Scanlan hit Joe Delmont with a 15-yard pass to the 11 yard line.

In the third quarter, another fumble gave Benilde the ball on the Cretin 19; they scored on an 18-yard pass, but missed the PAT. Benilde, 13, Cretin, 6. Following the Benilde touchdown and kickoff, Cretin had the ball on the Benilde 46 at the end of the third quarter.

Facing a fourth and 11 on the Benilde 48, Harren swept right end to the House, making it 13-12, Benilde.

Lining up for the all-important PAT, Harren stared down the goal posts. "I never thought of missing," he said. And he didn't. Dead center. 13-13, and that's the way it ended. @#@%%#.

Dick Harren did all the scoring for Cretin, rushing for two touchdowns and kicking one extra point. He ran for 188 yards on 14 carries, for a 13.4 yard average. In its game report, the *St. Paul Pioneer Press* newspaper called Harren "one of the best running backs in the state." We agree.

Next up, St. Thomas Academy. Against STA, the Cretin team was like a wounded bear, after suffering that ugly tie with Benilde. We pounded the Tommies, 26-6. Dick Harren, Mal Scanlan, Dick Paradise, and Steve Schmidt scored touchdowns for Cretin. **CHS**

HOCKEY

18-7

Champions
Central Catholic Conference

Cretin dominated the Central Catholic hockey scene during our four years there. We won the Minnesota Prep School Hockey Tournament five consecutive years, 1957-1960, and finished second in 1961 to St. Paul Academy (SPA), a team we beat 5-1 earlier in the year. Bummer.

In fact, Cretin dominated this league, winning 10 of the first 12 tournaments.

Minnesota's private and Catholic high school hockey teams were not allowed to participate in the Minnesota State High School League from 1949-1974 and so played their own tournament called the Minnesota Prep School Tournament. It combined the four teams from the Twin Cities Central Catholic Conference, the top four non-Catholic private schools, and Duluth Cathedral and Crookston Cathedral.

In 1961, Cretin was favored to win the state title again, after winning the Central Catholic Conference with an unbeaten 12-0 record. Cretin closed out its regular season with a 3-2 win over St. Agnes, as John Groebner poured in an unassisted goal with 17 seconds remaining. Mark Hoffman and Dick Haigh notched the other scores. Tim St. Martin had 22 stops in goal for Cretin.

Heading into the state tournament, Cretin's title chances looked very good. It boasted a 16-6 record with four of its losses coming at the hands of St. Paul Johnson (twice) and South St. Paul (twice), and the other two coming against perennial Minnesota powerhouse International Falls.

The games with IF were played in a tough—if unusual environment. The Broncos played their games across the border in Fort Frances, Canada. Brother Josephus was driving the Cretin bus and wasn't familiar with custom regulations, so he tore across the border heading for the arena without a second thought.

The red lights and sirens of the chasing border patrol soon got his attention, though. "Brother," the cop said, "you have to stop at customs. You can't just drive right through." Oh.

Cretin didn't have a lot of bucks for travel, so they stayed in a two-story motel that had seen its better days. "Our rooms were on the second floor," recalls Scanlan, "and the fire escape was a rope in each room. In case of fire, we were supposed to toss the rope out the window and climb down to the ground. Good idea, but the windows were all sealed shut. If there would have been a fire, we all would have cooked."

Cretin had beaten Benilde, St. Agnes and SPA during the regular season.

In the first game of the State Tournament, Cretin bounced Breck, 5-1, with Dick Haigh scoring twice and Mal Scanlan, Mark Hoffman and Gary Lievers scoring the other goals. St. Martin had 17 stops. In the second round, it edged St. Agnes, 2-1.

SPA nipped Cretin 2-1 in the title game on an odd goal in the third period with Cretin shorthanded. Dick Haigh was serving a penalty for catching the puck and tossing it into the crowd. SPA banged the puck home on the resulting faceoff to the right of the Cretin net, four seconds after Haigh left the ice.

"We lost that game," recalls Stewart, "and that was real, real disappointing. We were clearly the Number One ranked team in the tournament, and we lost that game."

Haigh scored at 10:24 of the third from Scanlan, when he circled the net and tossed the puck in the corner of the net on the partially screened goalie. St. Martin had 13 stops under heavy pressure after relieving Tom Haugh midway through the second period and coming up with nine saves in five minutes. Haugh had nine stops in the first period.

Even though Cretin lost the title game, six players made the All-State team: Mark Hoffman (defense), Tom Haugh (goalie), Mal Scanlan (defense-wing), Jim Stewart (wing0, Rick Smoliak (center), and Dick Haigh (defense-wing).
CHS

BASEBALL

5-2

Second Place
Central Catholic Conference

Undefeated Cretin faced St. Cloud Cathedral at St. Cloud Municipal Stadium in St. Cloud for the Central Catholic Conference title Sunday, May 20, 1961. Cretin had an exceptionally strong team, returning the entire starting nine from the previous year.

St. Cloud led in the opening game with its ace southpaw pitcher, Tom Burgmeir, and Cretin countered with hard-throwing Mike Hayes.

As Cretin took pre-game batting practice, Coach Warner told his team, "Don't worry about this guy. He's only got one pitch. Just wait on his fast ball."

That's just what Cretin's leadoff hitter did. Fastball—Strike one. Fastball—Strike two. Big sweeping curve ball. Strike three.

Walking back to the dugout, one could hear, "Fx@%%#. He's got at a curve ball too."

For the day, Burgmeir tossed a no-hitter and fanned 16 Cretin batters in seven innings, leading St. Cloud to a 1-0 gem. Hayes tossed a nifty one-hitter for Cretin. The loss snapped Cretin's 10 game victory string.

The only run was unearned and came in the first inning on a walk, a stolen base, a sacrifice fly and an infield error.

St. Cloud took the second game, too, 9-6, smacking 12 hits off three Cretin pitchers, while the St. Cloud hurler scattered five hits and struck out nine. **CHS**

BASKETBALL

12-10
Second Place
Central Catholic Conference
Regional Champion
Fourth Place, State Tournament

Cretin opened the 1961 Minnesota State Catholic Basketball Tournament at the St. Paul Auditorium blasting Marshall Central 61-44, led by Gary Droubie's 16 points and Jim Clarkin's 14 points. Marshall played tough in the first quarter and led 16-15, but Cretin's Bob Ryan stole the ball and drove the length of the court for a quick two points to open the second quarter. The game was close through the first half, with Cretin holding the first half lead 23-21, after shutting down Marshall with only five points in the second quarter. Cretin took control in the third quarter, running off 17 straight points, and outscoring Marshall 25-7.

In the semi-final game, Cretin used a tough defense to shut down De La Salle's high scoring ace Mike Gleason, holding him to only four points before finally losing 42-36. Tom "Whitey" Enestvedt led the defensive charge on Gleason, the tournament's most valuable player.

Coach Bill Tierney introduced a surprise defense against De La Salle—a four man zone with Enestvedt playing a tight man-to-man on Gleason. It worked. Enestvedt held the Central Catholic Conference scoring champ to his lowest scoring effort of the year with only one field goal in the third quarter and one in the fourth quarter. Gleason was able to get off only eight shots the entire game.

The Raiders were down five points at half time, 26-21, but came storming back to tie the game at 29-29 in the third quarter before the Islanders pulled away for good. De La Salle won the title the next day, beating Duluth Cathedral 74-58 behind Gleason's 32 points.

Cretin lost the final game to Mankato Loyola, 60-42. Droubie was named to the All-Tournament Team. **CHS**

Scoreboard, 1960-61

FOOTBALL
8-0-1

47	Lindstrom-Center City	6
39	St. Paul Academy	0
39	Fargo Shanley	6
31	St. Cloud Cathedral	13
13	De La Salle	6
13	Benilde	13
27	St. Thomas Academy	6
31	Murray	0
31	Austin Pacelli	12

HOCKEY
18-7

5	West St. Paul	2
2	De La Salle	1
7	St. Agnes	0
6	Alexander Ramsey	3
5	Hill	0
2	South St. Paul	3
5	SPA	1
7	Benilde	3
0	Johnson	7
8	St. Cloud	0
3	Benilde	2
3	De La Salle	1
5	STMA	0
6	Harding	3
2	International Falls	6
1	International Falls	8
3	St. Agnes	2

Tournament

5	Breck	1
2	St. Agnes	1
1	SPA	2

BASKETBALL

12-10

Cretin		Opponent
32	Benilde	40
45	Mechanic Arts	50
60	St. Cloud Cathedral	57
42	Central	50
42	St. Thomas Academy	40
37	De La Salle	63
76	Hill	49
42	Mechanic Arts	29
40	Benilde	38
52	Monroe	33
73	St. Cloud	53
52	Harding	65
52	St. Thomas	36
32	Harding	40
51	De La Salle	62
32	Central	54
54	Hill	32

Regional Tournament

71	St. Bernard	44
43	St. Thomas Academy	41

State Tournament

65	Marshal Central	44
36	De La Salle	42
47	Mankato Loyola	60

CHS

Intramural Sports

There were only 44 guys on our varsity football team but there were more great athletes in our class who played in our intramural leagues every week. The leagues were organized by Advisory, six teams in each sport. We played softball in the spring, football in the fall, and basketball or volleyball in the winter.

Quite a few guys played intramurals. Just look at the listings in the Cretinite '61 Yearbook. In Softball, there were 10 guys on a team. Teams played right after school, and players changed in the hallways by their lockers. Not very fancy.

Don Wolkerstorfer: "I played intramural football and softball all four years and really enjoyed them. I think a lot of guys played intramurals."

There weren't any championships with trophies, but that didn't matter. Everything was pretty loose and friendly that way, but competition got pretty heated at times.

"I enjoyed Intramurals a lot," recalls Wolkerstorfer "Also, Intramurals were not overly time consuming with respect to practice." **CHS**

Academics/Science

We had only been in class a few days when the Russians stunned the world with the launch of their Sputnik satellite on Oct. 4, 1957. It kicked off a revolution in science education in America when we saw how far behind the world we were.

Don Wolkerstorfer remembers that Sputnik got him thinking that perhaps there might be a career for him in science. He was correct. After earning a PhD in Applied Physics from Stanford University, he spent 32 years at the Los Alamos National Laboratory in Los Alamos, N.M., working in areas of national defense. Don was assigned to the Pentagon for two years where he worked with the Russians on helping them ensure the safety and security of their nuclear weapons after the collapse of the Soviet Union.

Al Broz was another successful graduate of the Cretin science program. Al earned a PhD in physics from Notre Dame University and worked for many years at the FAA as the Chief Scientific and Technical Advisor.

John Mueller earned a degree in Chemistry from the University of Minnesota as well as an MBA in marketing while working at 3M. John rose to become a top vice president with global responsibilities while working for 3M in Chile, Japan and the UK.

Mentored by Bro. Francis, the Science Club included some of the smartest guys in our class, several of whom earned a PhD in science or a medical, law or engineering degree.

In addition to Wolkerstorfer, Broz and Mueller, there were many other Classmates who were leaders in their professions. For example:

Dr. Gary Francis, is an internationally recognized cardiologist and is Professor Emeritus of Medicine at the University of Minnesota. He has published more than 560 scientific papers and has edited or co-edited 23 books. His work has been cited more than 50,000 times in the scientific literature, placing him in the top one percent of all scientists internationally.

Charles Reischel, Class Valedictorian, Cadet Colonel, Class Vice President and award-winning football player, graduated from Harvard College and Harvard Law School. Chuck was the chief appellate lawyer for the District of Columbia for 23 years, and he was named 2003-2004 Lawyer of the Year by the DC Bar Association.

Tom Horak earned a PhD in education and served for 13 years as president of Normandale Community College in Bloomington, MN.

John Biebel moved to Tampa Bay in 1982 as CEO of St Joseph's Hospital, one of the leading hospitals in the Tampa area, and subsequently adding three additional hospitals, and launched BayCare Health System. BayCare has grown into the largest health care provider on Florida's west coast with 18 hospitals, including 45 multi-specialty clinics and a myriad of home health services.

Louis Bushard, PhD, who earned his doctorate in mathematics at the University of Minnesota and then helped develop the Three-Mile Island Nuclear Power Plant. His career include time at Unisys, Cray Research and IBM during which he earned 16 patents.

Also making their marks academically and professionally were classmates such as Len Kohenen, Larry Lutton, John Lamey, Paul Ossmann, James Wiberg, Joe Steger, Terry Schulte, Doug Schwartz, Gordon Granse, Robert Buelow, Joel Montpetit, John Mayer, Bob Magnuson, Jerry Holmay, Jerry Hirsch, Dick Hammel, Mike Haider, Jerry Filla, and Bill Kuhns.

Look in the Appendix for other top academic performers who won school awards, scholarships, or National Honor Society recognition.

When we were in school, the roads for the local Interstate Highway system were being constructed. I-94 headed East and West through the former Rondo neighborhood and I-35E ran North to Duluth and South to Texas.

I-35E on the East Side of St. Paul was nothing but a cleared right of way at the time, but it made a perfect area for launching rockets. Dan Hayne, who lived in the area and whose father worked for the Highway Department, showed classmates the possibilities of launching rockets on that stretch of open area. And that's where guys from the Rocket Club and the Science Club settled in. **CHS**

Girls/Schools

There were no girls at Cretin during our tour of duty there, but we knew where to find them, and they knew where we lived. In 1960, there were four all-girl schools located within three miles of Cretin with a total student population of 1,963 ladies: Our Lady of Peace (OLP) (880), St. Joseph's Academy (752), Visitation (164), and Derham Hall (167). St. Agnes, a co-ed school located four miles away, had a total enrollment of 502, with a few hundred more ladies. We had plenty of prospects, but most of us didn't know what to do with them.

Our Lady of Peace high school was the top target for many of us.

At 3:00 each day, we poured out the front door and headed for our cars. It was a three minute drive north on Hamline Avenue to Summit Avenue, and then we'd hang a right on Summit. A quick two-minutes later we would turn left on Milton Street and pull up in front of OLP, where we would wait on Portland Avenue for the ladies to come out of school.

"When we finished class," said one lady, "we would walk back to our advisory and look out the windows to see if our ride was waiting. We weren't supposed to do that, but we did it anyway."

OLP was arguably our Number One source of dates— our feeder system, so to speak—but we also hooked up with girls from St. Joe's, Derham and Visitation.

St. Joe's was only a short drive from OLP and Derham was on the campus of St. Catherine's College in Highland Park, about two miles south of Cretin. DH built a new facility adjacent to Cretin on Albert street, directly west of Cretin, in 1962 with 238 students, prior to the merger of the two schools in 1987.

Visitation was located about three miles away, before relocating in 1966 to Mendota Heights, adjacent to St. Thomas Academy. Those girls mostly ran with the STA guys.

We didn't have much to do with 140 girls at Villa Maria Academy because it was so far away, about 50 miles south on Hwy. 52, towards Rochester. However, we were bussed down there every year for a dance. Those were strange, and quiet solemn affairs, as I recall.

Villa Maria was a boarding school, and the girls generally came from exotic places like Chicago and Brazil and had lots of money and were pretty sophisticated, and we generally didn't know what to say to them or how to dance with them. As one Cretin man put it, "I might have been a bumpkin with them, but I didn't even know I was a bumpkin." The rest of us, I think, knew we were bumpkins in front of these women, and we could hardly wait to get back on the bus.

The competitive situation began changing in our early years at Cretin. Hill High School for boys was founded in Maplewood in 1959 and the co-ed Archbishop Brady High School opened in West St. Paul in 1964. Archbishop

Murray Memorial High School for girls opened down the street from Hill High School in 1958. The two schools merged to form Hill-Murray High School in 1971.

St. Thomas Academy, of course, was a long-time competitor, although a minor one. STA was founded in 1885 and opened a new campus in Mendota Heights in 1965. In 1960, it had 585 students,

Across the river in Minneapolis, we had the tough De La Salle High School. D's enrollment peaked at almost 1,700 in 1964. No wonder we had a tough time beating those guys in basketball.

Benilde High School opened in St. Louis Park in 1956 and in 1960 it had grown to 904 students. Benilde merged with St. Margaret's Academy in 1974 to form Benilde-St. Margaret's. **CHS**

Social Scene

We really didn't have an icon or a mascot, but if we did it might have been Jay Laramy's bright red 1960 Chevrolet convertible, the one that's featured in the 1961 Cretinite Yearbook. Remember? My wife, Bobbie, does. "I rode in that car with Jay," she reminded me as we researched this book. Yes, Dear.

A side note: You could have purchased that car new in 1960 for about $2,900. Today, you would have to pay well north of $55,000 for a refurbished one. I would buy one, if I could.

The car actually belonged to Jay's Mom, but he drove it regularly. When he had the car, he would stop a few blocks after leaving his house, hang a pair of giant fluffy dice from the rear-view mirror and swap out the standard wheel covers for a flashy set of "moon" covers. Jay was a very popular guy, when he drove that car.

Jay, with his buddies, Kirby Kennedy, Tommy Arend, and Gordy Granse, took the car out to the Minnesota State Fairgrounds in Falcon Heights one fine spring day to check out the new car models that were on display in the racetrack infield. Remember when the car dealers had showrooms on University Avenue and Grand Avenue, block after block? There wasn't room on the show floors to display all the new models and handle the crowds of gawkers, so they parked the cars in the racetrack infield at the Fairgrounds.

After the guys finished looking at the new cars, Jay thought it would be fun to take a spin around the racetrack in the Chevy. "So, I'm cruisin' around that track about 90 miles an hour, and one of the State Fair police caught us—'What the hell do you guys think you're doing? Get the hell out of here before you kill yourselves.'" End of ride.

Sensitivities were different in the '60s. In paging through the 1960 issues of the *St. Paul Pioneer Press* newspaper I found this piece from syndicated columnist Earl Wilson, who wondered in his column "Where Are The Nice Girls?" Wilson starts his column by asking, "Whatever happened to nice girls, anyway? Have you noticed this is the era of trollops on stage and in movies? We wouldn't have these female bums in our homes, but we rush off to see them…"

Wow. I wonder what Mr. Wilson would think of the ladies on cable channels today.

Even though in 1960 we didn't have any girls on campus, ours was a fairly lively social scene because we had so many girl's schools in the vicinity. And St. Thomas Academy was the only all boys school close to us, but we didn't consider them any real competition. **CHS**

Mixers. Our dating scene was very much informal and group-based. Not so much one-on-one dating, but rather group hang-outs. Dances at Cretin were called Mixers, because they were designed for boys and girls to mix, not really to date each other. But they were very popular.

The mixers were so informal that many of the girls would ride the city bus to Cretin for the event, planning to pick up a ride home at the dance. Can you imagine that scene today? Not going to happen, as they say. Back then, it usually worked, from what I hear.

Mary T: "We all went to the same proms, we all double dated, we all snuck across the Wisconsin border, you know, to do a little drinking on the Hudson side of the (St. Croix) river."

At that time, the drinking age in Wisconsin was only 18, compared to 21 in Minnesota and nobody really checked IDs for drinking age in Hudson.

Formal Dances. We enjoyed the usual formal dances— homecoming, prom, Senior Date Dance, etc., but we also had the Military Ball and we had opportunities to go to formal dances at the girl's schools as well.

Actually, there wasn't a huge wave of eager participation in these dances, as I recall. Many of the dates were "arranged" by the faculties of the two participating schools, and we escorted ladies we had never met.

And, in most cases, owing in large part to our lack of sophistication, we never saw them again.

Mike Wold's experience perhaps was typical. Mike, who lived in Maplewood, double-dated with Don Wolkerstorfer, who lived on the East Side of St. Paul for the Homecoming Dance one year. Mike drove, so he had to go from Maplewood to the East Side to pick up Don before they picked up Don's date, who lived in North St. Paul. It was pouring rain and Mike got totally lost as he drove to pick up his date, and they ended up lost somewhere in South Minneapolis.

"We were extremely late for the dance, about two hours late, and we only had about two dances." Adding a classy touch to the evening, the guys took their dates to the St. Clair Broiler restaurant after the dance. "We thought it was pretty cool, but they were wearing these beautiful dresses—I love the Broiler, but usually I would be there in my jeans. My date didn't think the Broiler was quite up to par.

So, it was kind of a miserable night. I don't think Don's date ever forgave me."

The OLP dances had a special atmosphere. We were required to say a prayer at the beginning of the dance. As one classmate says, "If you're in the mood, that kind of took you out of the mood pretty quickly."

The Charity Ball was held at the Prom in cooperation with St. Thomas Academy. The dance was a flashy affair put on by a local mothers' group and smacked of a debutante ball as each of the girls was introduced during the Grand March.

The dance was limited to officers and their dates. It looked to be a nice event from the pictures I saw. As an enlisted guy, I didn't qualify to participate.

Cretin also held a Senior Date Dance in the school gym and the annual Military Ball for officers and their dates. The 1961 Ball was held at the Leamington Hotel in Minneapolis.

Heading across the river to the Big City of Minneapolis for a social event was an exciting and memorable occasion. Who knew what could happen in that foreign land?

The informal Mixers were held in the school gym regularly, especially after football games. I believe we called them "Victory" dances, since we never lost a football game.

Thousands of area teenagers attended the mixers, according to reports in the 1961 annual Cretin Yearbook.

We were a bit rough around the edges, in terms of social skills, and most of the guys hung out along the wall, near the door where withdrawal was easy. Dancing with a girl really wasn't considered part of the mixer agenda for most of us. But some were more daring, such as Richard Callinan.

After hanging on the wall for a while, he finally got up the nerve to look for a dance partner. "The spotlight seemed to follow me across the floor as I trudged over to ask a girl from St. Joe's for a dance," he recalls. "My buddies huddled together, watching, anticipating a possible big break in my social life.

"I was nervous, really nervous, sweating—what would I say? Probably something stupid. Finally, I walked up to one lady, and said, 'Would you...?' She immediately said, 'No, thanks.' The walk back across the floor seemed to take hours. My initial risk-taking venture with girls, didn't go well."

Catholic Youth Center. On Sunday evenings, the Catholic Youth Center (CYC) in Downtown St. Paul buzzed with activity for both boys and girls. The guys I was with mostly played basketball in the gym, but some of the others actually mixed with the girls. As it turned out, there was more to these events than we knew. One of the senior priests at the CYC later admitted to molesting girls at the center and was subsequently shipped off to work in South America.

I believe the saying, "Things are never as they seem," applied to activities at the CYC.

Rich Peacha played a special role in the social life of many Cretin seniors. Rich had a stocky build and a heavy dark beard. We called him "Bear." Rich looked much older than his actual age, which proved to be a decided advantage when he walked into a liquor store and ordered up a case of beer. No ID checks for Rich, who became the group's Designated Buyer.

The Homecoming event shows how we tapped into the huge pool of girls in the neighborhood. Pat Wessel, from St. Joseph's Academy, was the Homecoming queen, and five other ladies served as princesses: Lynn Haag, Derham Hall; Roseann Shaughnessy, Visitation; Alison Hurley and Mary Maley, Our Lady of Peace, and Rita Fox, St. Joe's.

Since we drew from pretty ladies at four schools, we had arguably the most beautiful homecoming royalty anywhere!

The theme of the homecoming event held Sept. 23, 1960, was "Shatter Shanley," a call to defeat Fargo Shanley in our game Saturday night at Midway Stadium. We did just that, beating them 39-6, on a rainy day before about 2,500 fans. Mal Scanlan scored three touchdowns and Jim Stewart returned a kick-off 80 yards for another touchdown, before breaking his arm. He missed several weeks of the season. You can read the details in the Athletics Section.

Columbian Squires. The downtown Columbian Squires organization provided a social outlet for some Cretin students. The Squires was an international youth fraternity run by the Knights of Columbus for Catholic boys between the ages of 10 and 18. The KC Hall was located on Ninth Street and the Squires met there about once a month.

John Biebel was an active Squire, especially when it came to shooting pool in the basement with a crusty codger named Colie McDonough, who always played with a burning stogie in his mouth.

The Squires group was launched in 1925, but it was shut down in 2016. Its stated mission was "to develop young men as leaders who understand their Catholic religion, who have a strong commitment to the Church and who are ready, willing and capable of patterning their lives after the Youth Christ."

In announcing plans to shut down the Squires, the Church said, "Squire Circles in the United States and Canada is discouraged, since the Catholic Church has a desire to move youth activities from exclusive clubs into the local parish youth groups."

Now, I was not a member of the Squires, so I can't speak directly to its activities, but John Stevens, who was Chief Squire during our senior year, told me the group had a variety of activities, many of which might be called borderline. "Today, we probably couldn't get away with some of the things we did back then. We'd probably be arrested for that stuff today."

Maybe that's why the Church dropped the program.

One event was boxing night, where guys got in a ring and wacked at each other without much supervision. One fellow had Golden Gloves experience, but he was taken down handily by a Cretin guy whose dad was a professional boxer and who obviously had passed on a few tips to our hero.

The Cretin guy had two other noteworthy bouts, both behind the Malt Shop, across the street from Cretin.

One involved a husky football player who was picking on a little guy in the hall one day. Our boxer, who weighed about 135 pounds, stepped in.

"Why don't you pick on someone your own size?'"

"How about you?"

A time was set for the space behind the Malt Shop across the street from school, and at the appointed time, the two had at it. Our hero landed a few good punches, according to those on the scene, but the heavier guy won out, eventually as they closed in together.

Our favorite boxer had another bout, in the locker room, with an even bigger football player. That bout he won. So, his record was two wins and a draw, against bigger, more experienced guys.

Back to the Squires. The group actually put on several neat events, including mixers at the Knights of Columbus hall in downtown St. Paul, and at the Ford Union Hall on Ford Parkway in Highland Village. The dances drew crowds of more than 100.

They also sponsored a hayride at Eaton's Ranch in December of our senior year. I remember that one—it was a great time. I spent much of the evening with Bobbie Seidl, my future and current wife. We've been married 57 years.

The Ford Hall also was the venue for dances put on by other Cretin guys, who were looking to make some money, especially during Lent, when there were no officially-sanctioned dances. Generally, Ford Hall mixers were run pretty well, and no one was seriously injured in any of the fights that popped up.

Snipe Hunts. Our social activities weren't limited to dances. We also conducted Snipe Hunts. The one Snipe Hunt in which I participated was held down by the Mississippi River near Minnehaha Park.

A Snipe Hunt is an event in which boys and girls hunt for small birdlike creatures called snipes. The name comes from the strange, sniping sound the animal makes. The birds are hunted with paper bags which the hunter drops over the head of the unsuspecting snipe.

A Snipe Hunt is fairly simple and doesn't require much equipment. First, one identifies an area where snipes might reside. Then a group of teenage boys and girls go to the area, each carrying a paper bag with which to capture the snipes. The hunt starts when the boys go in one direction and the girls in another, each person quietly calling, "Snipe. Snipe," to attract the snipes. When a snipe is captured, the bird is brought back to the group.

My wife Bobbie recalls her first Snipe Hunt with me, a few girls and some Cretin guys.

"I'd never been on a Snipe Hunt before," she says, a bit unpleasantly. "I didn't know what a snipe looked like, and I didn't know what I would do with one if I caught it, but I figured, 'Well, what the heck.' We hunted for a while without any luck and then my girlfriend, Jackie, and I realized we were alone—everyone else was gone!"

I can't really tell you how that hunt turned out. You'll have to ask her when you see her.

Oh, in case you're wondering, you can find Snipe listed in Wikipedia.

Although <u>snipe</u> are an actual family of birds, a *snipe hunt* is a quest for an imaginary creature whose description varies.

The target of the prank is led to an outdoor spot and given instructions for catching the snipe; these often include waiting in the dark and holding an empty bag or making noises to attract the creature. The others involved in the prank then leave the newcomer alone in the woods to discover the jok*e*.

Need we say more? **CHS**

DINKYTOWN

In the Sixties, the area around the University of Minnesota was loaded with apartments, dorms, bars, restaurants and stores supplying all manner of collegiate needs. Bob Dylan lived in Dinkytown and started his musical career in the area's bars.

Nothing was more exciting for us than driving to the U down University Avenue, dropping the car in some cheap street parking and heading to the basement of the Valli, the Italian restaurant that featured live music and pretty good pizza.

St. Paul kids heading to the Big Time UofM across the river in Minneapolis for fun and beer on the weekend. You couldn't beat it.

Vescio's and the Scholar were two other popular spots in Dinkytown for Cretin guys and our dates. **CHS**

HIGHLAND VILLAGE

Downtown Highland Village, at the intersection of Ford
Parkway and Cleveland Avenue, was the center for a lot of
our after-school activities, since it was loaded with retail and
restaurants and was only two miles from school.

Some of us dubbed Bill Treacy the Mayor of Highland
Village because he spent so much time there. He managed
the Chicken Little shop on Cleveland while he was enrolled
at Cretin, and he continued do so when he went to college.

Chicken Little. Bill Treacy was manager of this popular fast food spot on Cleveland Avenue just north of the
Italian Village restaurant in Highland Village. He worked
his way through Cretin and college at this fry pit, and said
he really enjoyed it. For only 99 cents, you could get a half
chicken, French fries, roll and cranberries, at this chicken
shop. Rick Sands worked with Treacy cookin' up chickens
here.

Lucky Lanes. We often headed to this bowling alley on
Ford Parkway before stopping for pizza in Luigi's below the
bowling alley. Rick Sands spent some time painting murals
at Lucky Lanes.

Farther down Ford Parkway was the **Ford Union Hall**
where the Squires often sponsored their dances, except
during Lent. Dances during Lent were frowned upon, but
that didn't stop us. Treacy, Rick Sands, Jim Just and Chuck
Reischel put their heads together and organized a dance
at the Ford Hall. It didn't last too long because there was
an early scuffle broken up by Officer Walley, a St. Paul cop
who had the Highland beat. Treacy called it "a cc in a bottle." At any rate, the hall emptied out early.

Embers on Ford Parkway always was a popular spot,
and there were a number of these tasty burger joints around
town. You could buy a "large, properly-aged Sirloin Steak
Dinner—tender as butter—seared on our new broiler" for

only $1.95. We usually settled for the Emberberger or the Emberger Royal because they were cheaper. An Emberger Royal, the deluxe burger, was only 95 cents!

Coleman's was a more upscale spot on Ford Parkway, and we only used it for special, big-buck occasions. It burned to the ground one night, after falling behind on its bills. Shortly before the fire, one vendor suggested we "sit by the door" if we ate there. Insider info?

Cecil's, on Cleveland Avenue, was a popular spot for its Rueben Sandwiches, for take-out or eat-in in its crowded back room. It's still as popular today, even with my grandkids.

Italian Village. This is long gone, but it really was popular for Friday night pizza, even though we Good Catholics only ordered cheese pizzas, no meat on Friday. The Catholic Church thought we needed a little sacrifice in our life every week. Come on. The IV was located at the corner of Highland Parkway and Cleveland Avenue, around the corner from the Highland Theater. Very convenient.

Lee's had two spots in Highland—Lee's Pantry and Lee's Kitchen—and they seemed to be going head-to-head with Chicken Little. Lee's Pantry offered a ¼ fried chicken dinner with French fries, cole slaw, dinner roll and Honey, for 85 cents.

St. Clair Broiler, a popular spot on St. Clair and Snelling Avenue only three minutes from Cretin, was owned by the same people who owned the Lee's restaurants. It was a frequent stop because you could get a coke with two straws and the chocolate malts were out of this world. **CHS**

FAVORITE RESTAURANTS

We had several popular spots in Highland Village because it was so close, but we didn't restrict ourselves to the Village. There were several other spots around town that we hit regularly.

Carbone's Pizza was the most popular restaurant with our class. Although Cecil's, Italian Village, Embers and the Bridgeman's ice cream joints—one on Randolph and Snelling, a few blocks from school, and another in Downtown St. Paul on St. Peter Street—drew lots of votes.

The first Carbone's was opened at 680 East Seventh Street in 1954, the second on the West Side's Smith Avenue, and the third might have been on Randolph Avenue, near Cretin, SPA and St. Catherine's College. Today, there are 37 Carbone's stores in the Twin Cities. Prices change: In 1960, a large sausage pizza cost $2, today, it costs $16.13, after tax—a 700% increase.

Clark's Submarine Sandwich shop on University and Dale also was a popular place for a late night snack. It was the first real submarine shop in town. In 1980, you could buy one for $1.39. In 1980 there were 15 Clark's, but they were gone in 1991.

Other popular spots included Porky's drive-in on University Avenue, Sandy's drive-in on University and Lexington, and Paul Pierson's drive-in on Minnehaha in Minneapolis.

McDonalds opened its first restaurant in Minnesota on Snelling Avenue in Roseville across from the current Har Mar Mall in 1954. The second was opened a year later in St. Louis Park. In May 1961, McDonalds opened in West St Paul. The "All-American" meal was a burger, fries, and a shake for 45 cents (plus tax). A standard order that I remember filling often was three burgers, two fries, and two cokes for 88 cents (3 cents sales tax). Mar 8, 2015.

White Castle. This place was unique. The building was shaped like a…. White Castle, and it served little, sliders—cheeseburgers—for about 20 cents. There was one on Seven Corners, one on Rice Street and University Avenue and one on the corner of Lexington Avenue and University Avenue. Quick and cheap. And oh, so tasty.

NCO Club at Fort Snelling. In our junior year, we weren't old enough to drink in a public bar, but that didn't stop some of us. One favorite spot was the old red brick NCO Club at Fort Snelling—not to be confused with the more elegant Officers Club located across I-494 from the Minneapolis-St. Paul International Airport. The NCO Club, tucked back in the fort's residential area, was more like your shabby neighborhood bar on West Seventh Street.

I can't verify the facts about Cretin's participation at the Club, because, of course, I never drank there, but from what I'm told a Cretin guy—Jack—drifted into this bar one night and ordered an alcoholic beverage. The barkeep served it right up, no questions asked, and no ID checked. Not bad. Mixed drinks only cost about a quarter because it was a federal establishment and the fed's special rules applied. Even better than no ID.

Soon, our friend Jack and a few friends began stopping by on a regular basis. As one puts it, "We'd drop in for a whisky sour, or two, to loosen us up a little bit, before we would pick up our dates."

Truth be told, part of the fun was just being able to get away with it—the under-age drinking part. Again, I wouldn't know about that. **CHS**

Movies

We didn't have Netflix and Amazon in 1960 but we had plenty of movie theaters and drive-ins. We had the Highland Theater around the corner from the IV, the St. Clair on the corner of St. Clair and Snelling Avenues and the Grandview on Grand Avenue and Fairview. The Highland and the Grandview are still operating.

Other neighborhood theaters, now gone, included the West Twins in West St. Paul, the Astor on the West Side and the Mohawk Theater, also on the West Side, to mention just a few.

Downtown St. Paul was a mecca for movie theaters. And they even offered free parking. The area on Seventh Street between St. Peter and Wabasha streets was loaded with theaters—Paramount, RKO Orpheum, Riviera, Strand, World—where we could see such scintillating films as *College Confidential* with Mamie Van Doren and Conway Twitty, *Portrait in Black* starring Lana Turner and Sandra Dee, and *From the Terrace* featuring Paul Newman and Joanne Woodward. The "Next Big One" at the Paramount starred Marilyn Monroe in *Let's Make Love*. And, of course, *Summer Place*, with Sandra Dee. It was almost too much for a teenage boy.

Around the corner, on St. Peter and Seventh, was the big Bridgeman's where we stopped after a movie. This corner was the big bus transfer point from Highland to the West Side, West St Paul and South St Paul so we spent a lot of time waiting in Bridgeman's.

It was a great spot to meet the ladies from OLP, St. Joseph's and St. Agnes, who also were waiting for the bus. I always would look for my future wife, Bobbie, who would ride the bus down from Victory and Grand where she would catch it after leaving OLP.

The average movie ticket in 1960 was 69 cents. Even with our crumby part-time jobs we could afford lots of these dates.

When we started driving, we could head to one of the many drive-in theatres that offered movies in addition to a private place to park for a couple of hours with our latest date. They ringed St. Paul from Roseville, Maplewood and the East Side to West St. Paul and Bloomington. The films were a little bit hotter than in the theaters, showing such delights as *Carry On Nurse, God's Little Acre*, and *Suddenly Last Summer*. **CHS**

FAVORITE MOVIES-TOP 20 MOVIES

Rank	Movie	1961 Gross	Tickets Sold
1	101 Dalmatians	$102,399,701	148,405,363
2	West Side Story	$43,700,000	63,333,333
3	The Guns of Navcrone	$28,900,000	41,884,057
4	El Cid	$26,600,000	38,550,724
5	The Absent Minded Professor	$25,381,407	36,784,647
6	The Parent Trap	$25,150,385	36,449,833
7	La Dolce Vita	$19,500,000	28,260,869
8	Lover Come Back	$16,937,969	24,547,781
9	Gone with the Wind	$14,888,889	21,578,100
10	King of Kings	$14,483,352	20,990,365
11	Come September	$12,710,696	18,421,298
12	Flower Drum Song	$10,738,117	15,562,488
13	Blue Hawaii	$10,440,453	15,131,091
14	Babes in Toyland	$10,218,316	14,809,153
15	Judgment at Nuremberg	$10,000,000	14,492,753
16	Fanny	$9,996,178	14,487,214
17	Return to Peyton Place	$9,996,178	14,487,214
18	Breakfast at Tiffany's	$9,551,904	13,843,339
19	The Misfits	$8,200,000	11,884,057
20	The Hustler	$7,600,000	11,014,492
21	Pocketful of Miracles	$5,000,000	7,246,376

OUR FAVORITE SONGS

Favorite Songs-Billboard Top 10
1. Tossin' and Turnin', Bobby Lewis
2. I Fall to Pieces, Patsy Cline
3. Michael, The Highwaymen
4. Crying, Roy Orbison
5. Runaway, Del Shannon
6. My True Story, The Jive Five
7. Pony Time, Chubby Checker
8. Wheels, The String-A-Longs
9. Raindrops, Dee Clark
10. Wooden Heart, Joe Dow
CHS

The Last Word

We hope you enjoyed this book. We wrote it for ourselves, but we wrote it for you, too, so you would know what it was like to be at Cretin in 1957-1961.

We were fortunate to be Men of Cretin: To learn from the Christian Brothers, from the Lay Profs, from the Coaches, from the Military Instructors, and from each other.

We were fortunate to learn personal responsibility. To learn discipline. To learn ethics. And to learn to be winners.

We learned... We Are The Best.

In Academics. In Athletics. In Personal Relationships.

In Everything we did.

Every Day of our Life.

We Are The Best.

Cretin Class of '61.

Thank you, Gentlemen. **CHS**

Appendix

In Memoriam

As of July 23, 2022, 75 of our classmates have passed away. This book is dedicated to them.

James J. Ahiers (3.16.1943-10.21.2000)

Stephen T. Archer (7.28.1942- 9.22.2001)

Lee G. Baker (12.27.1943-11.5.2001)

James E. Beaudette (5.11.1943-7.24.2002)

William Brandt (2.3.1943-2.1.2022)

Alfred L. Broz (2.17.1943-8.26.2018)

John N. Burger (5.8.1943-10.7.2012)

Joseph M. Clysdale (5.28.1943-12.4.13)

Thomas L. Connolly (3.20.1943-10.12.2012)

Joseph M. Courteau (5.26.1943-3.14.1980)

Gary P. Cummings (2.6.1943-12.7.2008)

Eugene P. Daly, Jr. (7.29.1943-12.87)

Patrick J. Daulton (2.23.1943- 4.24.2020)

Robert Doffing (6.25.1943-3.7.2022)

Wayne R. Effertz (5.20.1943-9.1.94)

David E. Essling (12.9.1943-11.1.2012)

Thomas J. Fischer (5.21.1943-12.10.1999)

Robert M. Foley (1.14.1943-8.13.2008)

David L. Francois (9.15.1943-8.13.1963)

Peter M. Fritz (12.1.1942-9.21.2020)

Col. Stephen R. Gerlach, USA(Ret)(4.11.1943-9.11.2016)

Michael A. Guiliani (3.3.1943-8.6.2022)

George F. Griesgraber (4.16.1943-10.2.1962)

John H. Groebner (9.12.1943-1.3.2013)

James L. Hammer (10.17.1943-11.09.1989)

Paul E. Harris (1.25.1943-7.5.2021)

Thomas J. Haugh (1.17.1943-8.4.2017)

Donald G. Haupt (6.25.1943-6.12.1968)

Daniel C. Hayne (3.10.1943-11.25.2018)

Jerome B. Hirsch (2.19.1943-12.26.2020)

Mark C. Hoffman (1.19.1943-4.6.2007)

David J. Houle (4.29.1943-6.23.2020)

Kenneth E. Jepson (4.17.1943-7.4.2007)

Gordon C. Johnson (7.28.1943-2.11.2015)

Gregory J. Kline (11.19.1943-9.24.2004)

John A. Korlath (8.12.1943-7.7.2001)

Peter Korner (5.1.1942-12.31.2010)

Roger A.Kramer (8.12.1943-5.15.2022)

Stuart S. Krick (1.10.1943-2.25.2004)

Timothy J. Kuechenmeister (4.7.1943-6.3.2018)

Stephen D. Kuslich (4.9.1943-12.14.2004)

George C. Lamson (12.21.1943-1.29.1985)

John H. Larson (6.20.1943-8.10.1974)

John E. Lentsch (9.17.1943-6.6.1992)

Lawrence P. Lindberg (6.6.1943-3.17.1994)

Stephen J. Major (7.8.43-5.21.2022)

Robert J. McCormick (5.21.1943-3.13.1989)

Thomas D. McKeown (3.11.1943-11.13.2006)

Bruce W. McLagan (2.24.1943-11.16.2010)

Bernard R. Mersch (12.23.1943-12.9.2014)

Paul T. Miller (8.1.1943-11.15.2008)

Robert M. Mitch (12.2.1944-2.18.89)

Joel A. Montpetit (10.21.1943-10.13.2021)

Robert F. Moosbrugger (8.24.1943-12.26.2004)

Stanley A. Morzinski (11.20.1943-3.24.2008)

Michael J. Murphy (1.20.1943-10.3.2020)

John J. O'Brien (8.24.1943-4.16.1981)

John G. Powers (4.18.1943-1.28.2009)

James J. Raleigh (11.9.1943-9.15.1993)

Charles L. Reischel (5.8.1943-7.15.2003)

C. Daniel Riegel (1.20.1943- 2.17.1994)

Ronald H. Robert (9.5.1943- 8.22.2019)

Richard J. Sands (5.11.1943-7.29.2019)

Daniel M. Shiely (4.26.1942-8.16.14)

Michael B. Shomion (2.18.1943-7.2.2016)

Robert J. Smith (5.12.1943-2.11.1986)

Richard G. Smoliak (2.23.1943-2.25.2014)

William J. Stadtherr (1.6.1943-7.5.2000)

George G. Strasser (1.6.1943-5.20.2014)

John F. Tocko (1.10.1944-10.2.2021)

Bernard J. Toner (3.31.1943-11.9.2009)

Jerome M. Tschida (11.10.1942-3/27/18)

Paul C. Vasterling (7.13.1943-4.30.2021)

Paul D. Wilson (1.18.1943-10.19.2001)

CW5 Joseph J. Yanchar, (Ret) (6.21.1943-9.19.2021) **CHS**

Graduating Class

May 29, 1961

Valedictorian: *Charles L. Reischel*
Salutatorian: *Donald C. Wolkerstorfer*

Joseph J. Abel
Joseph Paul Achterling
James J. Ahiers
James W. Allan
Richard J. Arcand
Stephen T. Archer
Thomas Edward Arend
Donald L. Awe
James E. Baillon
Lee G. Baker
James E. Beaudette
John Biebel
Ronald M. Bierbaum
James B. Bossard
Charles E.Boyer
William Sheridan Brandt
Dale John Brinkman
Joseph Paul Broneak
Alfred L. Broz
Jerome L. Buchmeier
Robert F. Buelow II
John N. Burger
Robert C. Busch
Louis Bernard Bushard
James H. Callahan
Richard T. Callinan

Michael J. Cardinal
Patrick J. Cavanagh
George M. Cepress
Richard W. Chambers
Thomas Charbonneau
James J. Clarkin
Joseph M. Clysdale
Thomas J. Connolly
Joseph M. Courteau
John P. Crenshaw
Jerome A. Cromer-Poire
Duane S. Crosland
Gary P. Cummings
Joseph J. Du Bruzzi
Eugene P. Daly, Jr.
Patrick J. Daulton
James H. Davis
Joseph D. Delmont
Robert M. Doffing
John E. Dolan
Daniel T. Drake
Gary M. Droubie
Wayne R. Effertz
Leo Joseph Elm
Carl T. Enestvedt
William J. Englund

James L. Esser
David E. Essling
James D Faust
William Gary Faust
Jerome P. Filla
Thomas J. Fischer
Thomas Fleischhacker
Robert Michael Foley
John C. Ford
Gary S. Francis
David P. Francois
Peter M. Fritz, Jr.
Michael J. Gaiovnik
John Joseph Gardner
Robert G. Gaylord
Joseph M. George
Stephen R. Gerlach
Michael A. Guiliani
Ronald G. Goblisch
George E. Goswitz
Robert L. Gould
Gordon E. Granse
George F. Griesgraber
Joseph F. Griesgraber
John H. Groebner
Richard G. Gruber
Michael M. Haider, Jr.
Richard J. Haigh
Philip J. Hamer
Richard J. Hammel
James L. Hammer
Robert A. Hanson
Richard G. Harren
Paul E. Harris
Dennis B. Hauber

Thomas J. Haugh
Donald G. Haupt, Jr.
Michael J. Hayes
Daniel C. Hayne
Ronald M. Hebaus
Michael David Henly
Ronald J. Henningsen
Dennis R. Herzog
Jerome L. Hiniker
Jerome B. Hirsch
Jerome D. Hoffman
Mark Hoffman
Dennis A. Holland
Jerome J. Holmay
Thomas J. Horak
David J. Houle
Edwin H. Howe, Jr.
John J. Hurley
William J. Huspeni
Lawrence K. Jackson
Lawrence H. Jandrich
Pau J Jasmin, Jr.
Raymond F. Jensen
Kenneth E. Jepson
Gordon C. Johnson
James. A. Just
Joseph M. Keenan
Thomas Stephen Kelly
Gregory John Kline
Leonard J. Koehnen
Joel M. Koemptgen
Robert P. Komives
John A. Korlath
Peter Korner
Michael Joseph Kraft

Roger A. Kramer
Stuart Stephen Krick
Timothy Kuechenmeister
Richard M. Kueppers
William Henry Kuhns
Stephen Damian Kuslich
Dennis Joseph LaComb
John Daniel Lamey, Jr.
George C. Lamson
John R. Landy
Jay Michael Laramy
John Harold Larson
William John Latusky
James D. Lemke
John E. Lentsch
James G. Lethert
Gary A. Lievers
Lawrence P. Lindberg
William Arthur Long, Jr.
Michael Ray Louis
Lawrence LeRoy Lutton
Robert J. Magnuson
Patrick H. Mahoney
Stephen John Major
John Joseph Mayer
Mark Patrick Maykoski
James H. McArdell
Dennis Edward McArdle
Robert Joseph McCormick
Joseph Martin McElhone
Thomas David McKeown
Bruce William McLagen
Patrick J. McLaughlin
Donald Clifford Mellin
Bernard Richard Mersch

Thomas Barrett Mich
Peter H. Mielke
Paul Thomas Miller
Robert Michael Mitch
Thomas Hugh Moloney
Joel Allyn Montpetit
John Patrick Moore
William John Moore, Jr
Robert F. Moosbrugger
Stanley A. Morzinski
John James Mueller
Michael Joseph Murphy
Henry Nonnemacher, Jr.
Thomas Edward Nuebel
John Joseph O'Brien
Ronald Joseph Ofstehage
Paul William O'Gorman
Daniel Jeremiah O'Keefe
Arnold Norman Olsen
John William O'Reilly
Paul Malcom Ossmann
Lawrence Burton Parrish
Richard James Peacha
Robert Jacob Phillips, Jr.
Robert James Pierre
Kenneth Pietraszewski
John G. Powers
Daniel L. Probst
Richard J. Prokosch
William F. Quinn
James J. Raleigh
Daniel R. Rask
James H. Rebeck
Charles L. Reischel
G. Daniel Riegel

Ronald H. Robert
Mark E. Robertson
Daniel L. Rossow
R. Lee Runyon
Richard V. Rylicki
Timothy J. St. Martin
Richard J. Sands
Malachy J. Scanlan
Peter A. Schmitz
John J. Schneider
Lawrence Schreiber
John W. Schubert
Terrance A. Schulte
Douglas A. Schwartz
Michael F. Shaw
Daniel M. Shiely
Michael B. Shomion
Ewen P. Sich
Louis A. Sitzmann, Jr.
Dennis S. Sleeper
Michael J. Smith
Robert John Smith
Richard G. Smoliak
Arthur John Sommers
Woodrow J. Spitzmueller
William J. Stadtherr
Joseph M. Steger
John Thomas Stevens
James H. Stewart
Thomas A. Stifter

Richard W. Strandberg
George Ggregory Strasser
William J. Sudeith
Charles J. Tambornino
Michael A. Thomason
John Quinn Tierney
John F. Tocko
Bernard J. Toner
William Patrick Treacy
Bernard M. Troje, Jr.
David A. Troje
Jerome M. Tschida
Gary James Unze
Paul Charles Vasterling
John A. Vornbrock
John J. Walters
Richard A. Warren
James E. Wazlawik
George William Weimer
Michael F. Whisler
Paul F. Whistler
James John Wiberg
Paul Douglas Wilson
Michael William Wold
Donald C. Wolkerstorfer
Robert Joseph Wood
Joseph J. Yanchar
Dennis Michael Young
CHS

National Honor Society

James W. Allen
Charles E. Boyer
William S. Brandt
Alfred M. Broz
George M. Cepress
Patrick J. Daulton
C. Thomas Enestvedt
Jerome P. Filla
David P. Francois
John J. Gardner
Stephen R. Gerlach
Richard G. Harren
Jerome B. Hirsch
Thomas J. Horak
James A. Just

Robert R. Komives
Stephen D Kuslich
John R. Landy
William J. Latusky
James G. Lethert
Stanley A. Morzinski
John J. Mueller
Paul M. Ossmann
Charles L. Reischel
Malachy J. Scanlan
Joseph M. Steger
John T. Stevens
James J. Wiberg
Michael W. Wold
Donald Wolkerstorfer

Awards

Brother Damian Religion Medal.
For excellence in the study of Religion over a period of four years.

James J. Wiberg

Science Award.
For achievement and interest in Science, the Bausch and Lomb Honorary Science Award.

David P. Francois

Mathematics Award.
For achievement in mathematics, the Mathematical Association of America and The Science of Actuaries Award.

Donald C. Wolkerstorfer

Chicago Tribune Awards.
Awarded for leadership, scholarship and service to the community.

Paul Ossmann   *Thomas J. Horak*

American Legion Award
Excellence in military and scholarship.

Mark. C. Hoffman

Reserve Officer Association Award.
Excellence in military and scholarship.

Richard C. Harren

Sons of the American Revolution.
Excellence in military and scholarship.

Jerome P. Filla

Superior Cadet Award

Charles L. Reischel

Elks Leadership Award

Lawrence L. Lutton

Contributors

Many of our classmates and friends contributed to this book. They provided insights and memories through our discussion groups and through emails and phone calls. They also provided suggestions, tips and professional assistance. Without this group, it would not have been possible to produce this book. Thanks, everyone.

Bill Treacy
John Biebel
Ron Bierbaum
Len Koehnen
Gary Francis
Mal Scanlan
Paul Ossmann
Rich Peacha
Bob Hanson
Larry Jandrich
Tom Enestvedt
Jim Davis
Dick Haigh
Jerry Filla
Don Wolkerstorfer
Tom Horak
Dick Harren

John Landy
Jim Stewart
Mike Wold
Mike Haider
Ray Jensen
Mark Robertson
Jim Rebeck
Jim Wazlawik
Bill Kuhns
Bob Busch
John Mueller
Tim St. Martin
Dave Berrisford
Bobbie Delmont
Bob Walsh
John Stevens
Thomas Carbone

Sponsors

Publication of this book would not have been possible without the financial support of our sponsors. Thank you.

John Biebel

Joe Delmont

Tom Horak

Bill Kuhns

Paul Ossmann

Rich Peacha

Mal Scanlan

Mike Wold

Don Wolkerstorfer

Joe Delmont is an award-winning journalist and freelance writer. He has written for several national business publications, and he was a reporter and Business/Finance Editor at the *St. Paul Dispatch-Pioneer Press* newspapers. However, since he had all the answers as a teenager at Cretin, he never worked on the *Comment* newspaper nor the *Cretinite* yearbook. Perhaps he didn't have all the answers, after all.

Considering a Corporate History or Family Memoir?
Contact Delmont Books LLC

We'll design, write, and produce your special book,
One that perfectly fits your exact needs.

Let's talk today.
Joe Delmont   612.845.8091
joe@delmontbooks.com   www.delmontbooks.com

Made in the USA
Monee, IL
30 October 2022

16825187R00111